WOMEN OF FAITH
IN THE MARKETPLACE:
FINDING YOUR KINGDOM PURPOSE

DOTTY J BOLLINGER

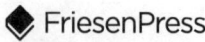

Suite 300 - 990 Fort St
Victoria, BC, V8V 3K2
Canada

www.friesenpress.com

Copyright © 2016 by Dotty J Bollinger
First Edition — 2016

All Scripture quotations, unless otherwise indicated, are taken from the Holy Bible, New International Version®, NIV®. Copyright ©1973, 1978, 1984, 2011 by Biblica, Inc.™ Used by permission of Zondervan. All rights reserved worldwide. http://www.zondervan.com/ The "NIV" and "New International Version" are trademarks registered in the United States Patent and Trademark Office by Biblica, Inc.™

All rights reserved.

No part of this publication may be reproduced in any form, or by any means, electronic or mechanical, including photocopying, recording, or any information browsing, storage, or retrieval system, without permission in writing from FriesenPress.

ISBN
978-1-4602-8492-6 (Hardcover)
978-1-4602-8493-3 (Paperback)
978-1-4602-8494-0 (eBook)

1. RELIGION, CHRISTIAN LIFE

Distributed to the trade by The Ingram Book Company

TABLE OF CONTENTS

Acknowledgments ix

Introduction xi

Chapter One:
Your Warrior Purpose 2

Chapter Two:
God's Plans Are Perfect 20

Chapter Three:
Reconciling the Proverbs 31 Woman .. 38

Chapter Four:
Loving Zacchaeus 52

Chapter Five:
Put On Your Listening Ears 74

Chapter Six:
The Jesus Card....................... 88

Chapter Seven:
Fitting In 102

Chapter Eight:
Juggling Act 118

Chapter Nine:
For Such A Wretch Like Me.......... 144

About the Author.................... 161

For my praying momma, Jane Sheldon, whose faith in Jesus Christ is the strongest I've ever known.

ACKNOWLEDGMENTS

My husband Jim—my best friend and lover—believes in me, supports me, and is my greatest cheerleader through thick and thin. He relentlessly encourages me to believe in myself and to see the potential in me that other people recognize. I can't imagine a life without his persistent support and encouragement.

I am thankful for our perfectly and wonderfully made daughters, Ashley and Sara, and for our son-in-law, Kevin. Being a mom is the best assignment I've ever had. I pray my children live the story God has entrusted to them while supporting, defending, and loving each other with all their might—all for the Kingdom of God.

INTRODUCTION

Women lead, submit, nurture, birth, fight, comfort, provide, and are provided for. God created each and every one of us. His creation includes those of us who seek His will and those of us who never give Him a second thought. He created believers and non-believers alike for a specific purpose: to benefit the Kingdom of God. Finding your purpose and living it to your greatest potential is what each of us is called to do. The Kingdom is especially dependent upon those of you who, like me, are strong female warriors of faith whom God has called to careers and ministry in the marketplace.

If you've picked up this book, you're likely a Christian working woman looking for someone to help you validate that what you're doing is right. You are probably a wife and a mother or planning to inhabit those roles. You make lunches, keep the house clean, get the kids to soccer practice on time, find a few minutes every day to have a grown-up conversation with your husband, are active in a church (or feel guilty that you don't attend one), all while working fifty hours a week outside the home. You're tired and surprisingly lonely in your fast-paced world surrounded by people. You have a passion for your profession, whether or not you need to work due to financial pressures, and you can't imagine a full-time life void of making a difference in the marketplace. And you're looking for confirmation that you are honoring God and that you aren't alone in your struggle to do so! While it feels like a heavy load, you have a special and important calling assigned to you by God. You are not alone. You join many strong, courageous marketplace leaders commissioned by God for such a time as this.

Jesus Christ is the Son of God. He came to earth as a baby, fully God and fully man to die for my sins—*my* sins. What a Savior! Because I have repented of my sinful nature and accepted Christ as my Lord and Savior, He walks before me and the Holy Spirit resides within me. When I abide in Him and seek His face, He speaks to me in ideas, dreams, and visions. Sometimes His voice is a whisper, and sometimes it's a shout. I find Him to be ever present when I decrease myself enough to acknowledge Him.

I am a conservative Christian with a business reputation as a powerhouse in the marketplace. I love to mentor and am a vigorous supporter of women in business. I have spent years seeking confirmation and approval from the church that it's okay for a woman to command a boardroom, be the primary breadwinner for a family, and love the Lord, all while honoring a husband who takes on a non-traditional role in the home. I am not a biblical scholar, but I love the Lord and seek guidance and encouragement in His Word and through the Holy Spirit, who is alive in me. My confirmation has come from the Lord alone that His creation in me is not an aberration. I have seen great and mighty works of His hand in the secular marketplace and have been blessed to understand that ministry takes place for each and every one of us exactly where our feet are planted—if only we are willing. Being a woman of faith called to live out ministry in the secular marketplace is not an easy road, but it is the challenge that inspires this warrior spirit to strive to do great and powerful things for the Kingdom of God. It is my hope this book will help you to see your "work" as your God-given purpose, calling, and ministry, and that you will leave inspired, refreshed, and recommitted.

The Lord has been so clearly present in the progression of my professional career. I believe He is seeking other women to be obedient in similar fashion, to "just get in the chair", and to trust that He will give all the gifts and talents needed to execute the strategies and ideas He will provide. My prayer is that you will find comfort in the knowledge that you are called to do great and mighty things for the Kingdom of God as you carry out your ministry in the marketplace, with God leading you every step of the way.

God is proud of His creation in you. You are made for Kingdom greatness. You can have everything He created you for! You are welcome here, and you are among friends. The time to live with focus and intention is now, so take your passionate, non-traditional warrior self and make a difference today in whatever God has called you to do. God created plenty of women who are more comfortable at the boardroom table than they are at a school bake sale. Let's fellowship with one other and work to mentor others so the next generation of working women of faith called to the marketplace know they play a very important role in the Kingdom. God creates strong women every day. He positions us in strategic places to bring others to His Kingdom and to be a light in a dark and fallen world.

When I was in law school, I interned for a healthcare organization whose general counsel, Matt Michels, was also the Speaker of the House of Representatives for the State of South Dakota. I could tell from my first day interning under him that Rep. Michels was smart, determined, and kind. Even though he was also an elected official, he didn't overtly broadcast his political party allegiance in the hospital workplace. As I was new to South Dakota, I didn't know what party he belonged to. One day I simply asked him whether he was a Democrat or a Republican. I've thought of his answer many times since. Mr. Michels said to me, "Worry less about political labels and more about using your God-given talents for the service of others." Those few words of wisdom would impact my professional planning for many years to come. God is trusting me with a story, and certainly he's given me talents that He intends me to use in the service of others. Any professional aspirations I would have would first begin with asking myself how my talents would effectively serve others.

After law school and a year of working at a traditional "Big Firm", I prayerfully took a break from the marketplace for about a year to wait upon the Lord and focus on my family. Jim's job had brought us to Chicago for a promotion, and I was determined to wait on the Lord and find my godly purpose while nurturing my girls as a stay-at-home mom. One hot summer day, I walked out of our suburban Chicago home with the girls and, dressed in bathing suits, we headed to the community pool. With a towel wrapped around my waist, my arms full of towels and toys, and two children in tow, we were on a summer day mission! Suddenly a car pulled up in front of us and stopped. In the driver's seat was a man I didn't recognize; he was wearing a business suit.

"Are you the healthcare attorney?" he yelled through his open window.

I nodded.

"My wife says I need to meet you to discuss my company. Are you available Saturday morning?"

Despite my embarrassment at meeting a stranger while I was half dressed, I somehow managed to tell him I would be happy to chat on Saturday. He handed me his address and drove off.

Ugh, did that exchange really happen while I was dressed in a bathing suit? I thought.

I had no idea what the context of the conversation would be, but on Saturday I donned a business suit and headed to his home a few blocks from ours, thinking he probably was seeking some kind of legal advice. He invited me to sit with him on the back porch. As soon as I sat down, a large orange cat jumped onto my lap. Now, I don't like cats; I'm allergic to them. However, as I'd been wearing my bathing suit at our first brief meeting, I was determined to make a good impression at this one, so I allowed the cat to settle in on my lap for a morning snooze.

We talked for two hours about his rising start-up healthcare management company and his need for someone with my resume to join his team. At the end of our time together, he offered me an executive position on his start-up team. He indicated he hoped I'd agree to begin right away. As I stood to leave, he asked if I was a cat lover. I confessed that no, I didn't actually care for cats, but I didn't want to insult his pet in his home. Surely God has a great sense of humor because my host said, "I have no idea whose cat that is."

I didn't understand it in these terms at the time, but my marketplace ministry began that day, right on that porch, holding a stranger's cat. As much as I was enjoying time at home with our girls, I knew in my heart that my calling was to the career that God had fashioned me for. After a time of reflection and consideration with Jim and the girls, we decided indeed this was a perfect and exciting professional opportunity. The timing was ideal: Sara was about to enter kindergarten, and Ashley had been enrolled in public school. The Chicago public school system indoctrinated their students with a liberal worldview, which didn't mesh with our principles, so this new job would allow us to enroll both girls in private Christian school. I can so clearly see the hand of God when I look now in the rearview mirror. He provided exactly what we needed at the exact time we needed it. We saw the blessings this position would provide for our family; later we would understand the greater Kingdom purpose as well.

While the rearview mirror is an accurate way to see the Lord's handiwork, you'll have more peace when you learn to walk with him in the present. I've grown professionally and spiritually since that cat-on-the-lap interview, and each day I strive to be adept at recognizing His voice and direction in the here and now. I'm confident, if you stay alert and listen, you too will hear God's voice. Instead of just seeing opportunities and circumstances as things that happen in day-to-day life, start considering them in the context of how God might be moving in your life. The scope and impact of your ministry may have no limits. I have had the privilege of encountering others in ways I could never have orchestrated but for God's favor and prompting. I also fear I've missed so many opportunities to minister to others because I didn't listen with an open heart and mind. Fortunately, every day is a new opportunity to listen to the prompting of the Holy Spirit as you walk out your kingdom purpose in the marketplace.

As I poured through my notes and journals to remember all the ways the Lord has provided faithfully during my marketplace journey, I was encouraged and amazed at the scope and consistency of the Lord's provision. Sometimes I was in a season of faithful fasting and study and He would show up in big ways; at other times I was overwhelmed with business pressures and could see evidence that I wasn't as faithful (e.g., having weeks where I missed making journal entries), but still God was present and provided great reminders of His faithfulness. When we seek Him, we find Him. And when He calls us to a purpose and we desire in our heart to follow His ways, He provides—even in our weakness.

Your marketplace calling may well allow you to send your children to private school, but that's not the only reason for the assignment. We are threads in the tapestry that the Lord is weaving to advance His Kingdom. I've seen the Kingdom advance through ministry to women in the workplace in powerful ways. One of my favorite encounters was during an early morning meeting with a woman twenty years younger than me who was in charge of a local charity. I hadn't met her previously, but a peer had asked me to take the meeting. I'd agreed, even though I knew I'd be asked to join some committee and would probably be asked for money.

This young woman entered my office right on time that morning and began, in a very professional manner, to recruit me to her cause—and of course, she sought my partnership for fundraising. I thought about how many people came to me with the same request for time and money, and my mind wandered to whatever was next on my agenda that day. However, the Holy Spirit quickened in me, and I felt in my spirit that this woman came to my office that day in need of encouragement. I interrupted her presentation, and without any context (because I didn't know anything about her), I just started chatting with her. I told her a story about how difficult it had been for me as a working woman when I was her age, and how it sometimes felt impossible with small children at home, not to mention getting them out of the house on time. I told her I admired her because I could imagine she struggled with conflicting feelings about seeking a profession versus staying at home with her kids. I explained how I came to recognize that I was called to the marketplace and that my career was actually my ministry assignment. I told her somewhere along the way that the Lord had allowed me to understand that I was called to be mother, wife, *and* a career professional. I let her know He always provided the way to walk out my purpose when I maintained my focus on Him.

As she listened intently, she quietly wept. She told me she was a believer and was feeling completely at the end of her rope that particular morning. Nothing seemed to be going right for her on that day; she felt like a failure and was now completely overwhelmed at the Lord's grace that He would provide her with confirmation that she was not alone. God knew her struggle was real.

I don't remember if we completed our business discussion during that meeting (we would have several over the next few years). I do know that as sisters in Christ we bowed our heads and prayed about the burdens she was carrying that particular day. She left my office encouraged. The Creator of the Universe cared for her in a very personal way. What a gift for any of us to know we're not alone. That day we became sisters in Christ and friends forever. And I did partner with her in her professional endeavors by joining her philanthropic committees and assisting with fundraising and community efforts.

So much of what we need to be effective day after day as working women of faith revolves around encouragement and community. The first step to being successful in your calling is to understand that you are not an anomaly. We are not alone. The Holy Spirit from time to time gives me a gift of discernment to identify women in the marketplace who are in need of this "sister" connection for the purpose of building up the Kingdom of God. "Use your God-given talents for the service of others," as Mr. Michels had exhorted me. For some of us, our talents are highlighted in the workplace.

I know how to lean in, give a hand up, stand up, speak up, and all those other things that working women are supposed to do to be successful in the workplace. I also understand how important it is that I help other women do those things as well.

You, plus God, are a powerful force to be reckoned with. We are incredibly lucky to have been born women in the United States at this time in history. There are more opportunities for us than for any other human beings on earth. We can demand equal rights, we can fall into traditional female roles, and we can give birth to children or choose not to have any. No door is closed to us. We can be anything we are called to be and have everything we are meant to have. As women, we are highly intuitive with a natural tendency towards advocacy and nurturing, making us unique, complex beings capable of delivering greatness. We have a multitude of opportunities and choices.

But you can't have it all. Yes, you read that correctly—you can't have it *all*. What is "all" anyway? Freedom? Structure? Relationships? Independence? Children? World travel? Courage? Comfort? You can't have all the things of this world. And you were never intended to. Neither was anyone else, least of all those women who tell you they think they actually *do* have it all. You *can* have exactly what God intended for you, including everything and everyone you need to fulfill your God-given purpose on this earth. Until we grasp that concept with full understanding, as women of faith we run the risk of burying ourselves with guilt as we strive to do too many things well and end up doing most just mediocre.

You may be trying to reconcile your calling to the workplace with the Word of God. If so, you need a special kind of support, encouragement, and direction. God certainly created strong women with loud and intentional voices to promote the causes of women in society and in the workplace. And those qualities are not an anathema to loving the Lord, praying without ceasing, or supporting your husband as a good and loyal wife. Sometimes the Holy Spirit will cause you to lean in. Sometimes He will full-out lead you to "just get in the chair", and he'll drive every business strategy and decision you need while you're there. And sometimes he'll call you to be different than what you may think society says is the norm for a Christian woman. You are a strong-willed, smart, gifted, driven woman who loves the Lord and who desires to do His will first. God has called you to make a big impact on the world from the place of business.

One of my primary warrior purposes is to encourage Christian women called to the workplace to embrace their important calling, to be successful, and to support others who are similarly spiritually situated. My godly purpose fits me well. As far back as I can remember, I've always felt a little bit different, rebellious, and misunderstood. My earliest memories include fighting for the downtrodden, the underdog, and others who didn't think they fit in. Somewhere along the way I picked up the label "warrior", and I've worn this label for years with great honor and distinction. It accurately captures my spirit for going to battle to fight for what is right.

Take a step back. Breathe. You are not simply a woman of faith who happens to work outside your home. You are a warrior for the Kingdom. Start thinking of your entire life, home, and work as your ministry. Your obedience to God's calling to the marketplace will bless many. Your success in the marketplace and the daily decisions you make will advance the Kingdom by opening doors and providing opportunities for others. The Kingdom of God needs you to fulfill your calling. To encourage you as you embark on this path, I'll open each new chapter with a Bible verse, share testimonies from other women who have sought out their ministry in the marketplace, and provide you with an opportunity to reflect at the end of each chapter by asking a few pertinent questions. Find a friend to read this book with, and I pray you may be doubly blessed.

There is no greater satisfaction than living smack dab in the middle of where God intends you to be! May your heart be strengthened to embrace God's plan for your life.

Have I not commanded you? Be strong and courageous. Do not be afraid; do not be discouraged, for the LORD your God will be with you wherever you go. (Joshua 1:9)

Be shepherds of God's flock that is under your care, watching over them, not because you must, but because you are willing, as God wants you to be; not pursuing dishonest gain, but eager to serve. (1 Peter 5:2)

CHAPTER ONE:
YOUR WARRIOR PURPOSE

For you created my inmost being; you knit me together in my mother's womb. I praise you because I am fearfully and wonderfully made; your works are wonderful, I know that full well. (Psalm 139:13–14)

And we know that in all things God works for the good of those who love him, who have been called according to his purpose. (Romans 8:28)

What impacted me the most was how everyone knew her heart for the Lord by the way she made decisions and cared about people. She didn't have to walk around the office thumping a Bible or preaching fire and brimstone; she taught the Gospel in a very real way, a way that even the world could understand and a way that encouraged all other believers around her in our workplace to step up and do the same. It was a subtle but very bold and loud kind of Christian leadership. She helped me see that strong Christian women don't just need to be at home raising children but rather that God calls some of us to the corporate world to make a difference in the lives of those with whom we rub shoulders. She often reminded me to work hard, to be the best I could in my assignments, and to dare to boldly let others know who I am in order to have an impact on the Kingdom while doing it.

—Lora I.

I SPENT YEARS FEELING GUILTY ABOUT MY desires to be successful in the marketplace. Perhaps you can relate. As I sought business success, I secretly thought real women who loved the Lord stayed at home and cared for family. I didn't find clarity in my purpose until I sought it directly from the One who assigned it: my Savior Jesus Christ. It's wonderful to be a child of God. It also can be overwhelming to be a child of God who has a huge to-do list, balancing home, family, friends, and work. Do you wonder what you were designed for? Why God created you? And whether or not you're being obedient to Him in the way you're living your life? You can find immediate comfort knowing that God didn't create you for busywork and an overwhelming to-do list that spans several pages. He created you for a special Kingdom purpose, with skills, desires, and abilities that are yours alone. Your obedience in fulfilling your purpose is the honor that awaits you as you seek His direction for this assignment created for you and you alone.

God created you for a purpose that is special and unique. When you focus on discovering that purpose and relying on Him to guide you as you carry it out, you'll come to realize that obedience is a much lighter load than the busyness that we create in our own world when we move day by day without intention and purpose. You'll find a great sense of peace that only comes from being in sync with the Creator of the Universe. As a woman of faith who feels drawn to the marketplace, there are a multitude of forces that come against you to confuse you and make you question your obedience to the Lord. The isolation that comes to believers who take the road less traveled doesn't have to persist. God created many women for marketplace assignments. You're going to be surprised where you find others in your workplace setting when you begin to ask the Lord to reveal them to you.

I love the Lord. I am strong-willed, intelligent, gifted with insight, prophetic, wise, and tenacious. I'm not particularly nurturing in the traditional sense. I adore my children more than life itself, but I wasn't a mom on the floor playing dolls or kissing booboos. I was the one encouraging them to shake it off and get back in the game, always encouraging bigger dreams and bigger assignments! I was drawn to a professional work environment even from a young age. Every job I had inspired me to work hard to be promoted. I used to believe all these qualities made me different; a woman with what the world taught me were "male" character traits. Once I started gaining opportunities to mentor and influence women in the workplace, I realized many other women felt exactly the same way I did and that a surprising number of them were believers.

We not only shared our passion to make a professional difference, we also shared our feelings of guilt and wondered if we were being faithful to God while pursuing business goals. Only when I started to understand that my career giftings were talents meant to be used for ministry and service unto others did I truly begin to understand my marketplace calling and my Kingdom purpose.

According to the U.S. Department of Labor's most recent data, 57% of women over the age of 16 contribute to the workforce in the United States today. That's a lot of working women. I'm guessing that a large percentage of these women feel overwhelmed on a frequent basis, juggling family, work, and community responsibilities. And for those who are believers in Christ, add in some good old-fashioned guilt that perhaps Christian women are supposed to be at home tending to family and not in the marketplace at all. God creates strong women, and many of us are designed to be career women. You are not alone if you are conflicted regarding your passion for work and whether or not that's a godly quality. Generally speaking, our churches are not overtly supportive of women called to the marketplace as ministry—just check the schedule for the women's ministry times to determine that! You were created by God to make a huge impact on the world for the advancement of the Kingdom. Our lives are to be lived in ministry, wherever we find ourselves called. As a believer and a working woman, your marketplace assignment is your ministry. God doesn't give you a Kingdom assignment and then carve out time from your assignment where you can go ahead and serve the world. Every breath you take and every ounce of energy you expand is to be intended for the glory of God. If your assignment is in the marketplace, that assignment is your ministry and that venue is your mission field.

A few years back, I was asked to speak at a non-partisan professional women's conference on the topic of mentoring women in the workplace. As I sat in the audience waiting my turn to give my speech, I was struck by the audience's response to the keynote speaker. She was a retired liberal politician, who with animation and vigor delivered an enthusiastic speech full of liberal women's viewpoints. That wasn't a surprise to me—it was, after all, a working women's event. I'd expected the audience to lean politically to the left. What did surprise me was that while she was energetically delivering her message, only half of the audience was responding enthusiastically to her. The other half was sitting back, not applauding, not cheering, and not reacting in any way. It was an "aha" moment for me. The lack of reaction to her led me to believe that half of this room full of women likely held conservative views regarding women's social and fiscal issues. But these conservative women shared an important interest with their liberal-thinking peers.

WOMEN OF FAITH IN THE MARKETPLACE

Each of the women in the room was seeking to be successful in the marketplace—that's why they were in attendance at a working women's conference. They were seeking advice, fellowship, and guidance from other women. I couldn't stop thinking about the disconnect between this liberal presenter and half the room. By the time I took the stage, I had forgotten about my mentoring topic. Instead I began my own rant on the power of a room full of women if we could agree to focus on subjects in the middle of the political spectrum and not just those squeaky issues all the way to the right or to the left. Fortunately, the speech was met with a lot of enthusiasm as the room considered our common ground. By God's prompting, because of my remarks that day I was asked to share a stage with Florida's Governor Rick Scott as he made a re-election campaign stop on women's issues a few days later. Apparently finding an outspoken conservative female business leader who would stand openly with a conservative governor wasn't easy to find, and I was honored to oblige.

I left that working women's conference with a new understanding that as a successful, outspoken Christian woman in the business world, my conservative thinking was not as aberrant as I'd always believed. I hypothesized that in most rooms full of career women, half were likely to hold firmly planted conservative worldviews that they probably kept to themselves because the world expected them to hold the opposite ones.

How many of these women considered themselves Christians? How many of them viewed their work as their ministry? How many of these women choose not to raise their voices in rooms like these because they didn't believe they'd be accepted? How many wondered if being in the marketplace was approved by God? Thankfully, my faith journey has taught me that I can love the Lord, honor my husband, nurture my children, *and* make a great Kingdom impact on the world as I fulfill my God-given purpose in the marketplace. I left that conference with a new understanding and a new mission: at least half the room would appreciate knowing they are not alone.

> **For we are God's handiwork, created in Christ Jesus to do good works, which God prepared in advance for us to do. (Ephesians 2:10)**

What did God create you for? Broadly speaking, you are created to love and worship Him; specifically, you are called to love others as yourself, in the unique way He created you to do that. God created you with a unique personality. Perhaps you have quick insights, a great sense of humor, a keen attention to detail, or other special traits. However you were formed, you are perfectly and wonderfully made, to do great and wonderful things. When you seek direction from the Lord, consider the deepest desires of your heart, ponder "circumstances" that brought you to this place, and begin to think of your life as a ministry field. You'll discover a confidence and *peace* that only comes when using all your gifts and talents to fulfill your God-given purpose.

Why are you in the marketplace? Think about the circumstances and desires that brought you to where you're planted today. Consider your earliest desires and dreams. Are the two in any way related? Do you remember dreams and aspirations from your youth that correspond in some way to your current workplace assignment? Begin to ask the Lord to reveal to you the Kingdom assignment he's reserved for you. Pray for discernment and clarity about what He might be telling you. It's okay to dare to say it out loud as you explore God's truths for your calling, even if it sounds funny! There's nothing wrong with loving the Lord your God with all your heart and all your soul while striving to lead a Fortune 500 company or writing a book or starting your own company if you think that's what He's calling you to do. You were created for a purpose all your own, and the Kingdom is counting on you to fulfill it.

> **The purposes of a person's heart are deep waters, but one who has insight draws them out. (Proverbs 20:5)**

Your God-given purpose has been inside you all along, waiting to be born and lived out. You were created in the image of God with a calling that is only for you. You spend your entire life with this purpose, whether you face it head on, take a few side roads, meet with the enemy's distractions to thwart it, or ignore it altogether. We're all created for a purpose, believers and non-believers alike. I'm a firm believer that each of us innately knows or will be shown our God-given purpose if we seek to find it. Our advantage is that as believers, we have the Holy Spirit to guide us and provide us wisdom and discernment regarding our plans. What did you dream about as a little girl? I bet you'll find you see a hint of your greater purpose there.

I used to dream of being a secretary to the "man who ran a big company in a big building in a big city". What's interesting about that dream is that I was raised in a small rural community with no access or real knowledge of what a big city was. My father was a blue collar laborer and my mother stayed at home. We lived on a small farm and rarely traveled more than 50 miles from our home. We had a television with only one channel, and my mother limited our viewing. To say I was sheltered was an understatement. Yet I saw myself serving the most important person in a big high-rise office building. I dreamed that my role would be key to the company's success. I would many years later understand the Lord had planted these seeds of marketplace Kingdom purpose in me. Decades later, I would find myself at the top of the corporate ladder, ultimately serving in different key roles in various emerging growth companies. In these executive positions, I served the various heads of companies and boards of directors in roles very important to the company's success. Reality surprisingly mimicked those foreign dreams and visions of my three-year-old self many years before.

Don't get me wrong—I didn't have a dream as a child and neatly and intentionally partner with the Lord as I grew up to live out this purpose. While that would have been neat and concise and well-planned, it wouldn't have been consistent with my journey of growing in relationship with the Lord. I nearly always took the harder road. I based my career aspirations on my practical needs, thinking little of those dreams and aspirations I held in my heart. I earned a degree in nursing for practical reasons. There was a nursing shortage in the United States when I was heading off to college, and I knew heading into that field of study I would always be able to get a job. I knew it would be a career that I could excel in financially, and it would provide me flexibility of work hours, since healthcare is a 24/7 industry. It was, for all practical purposes, a good idea. However, while I was seemingly headed out with my own agenda many decades ago, in the rearview mirror I see clearly how God was always there. My dreams and aspirations were always there too, deep inside me. God traded my ashes for a crown of beauty (Isaiah 61:3). He merged His marketplace purpose for my life with my career choices, knowing that eventually I would acknowledge His greater calling for my life and seek His direction. Thankfully, my own plans and choices didn't derail God's Kingdom purpose. Yours won't either. If you seek Him, there's nothing you've done or any step that you've taken that God can't work with (or overcome) in order to further his Kingdom and set you firmly in the middle of your purpose.

> **You armed me with strength for battle; you humbled my adversaries before me. (Psalm 18:39)**

Even in the 21st century, it's hard to be a woman working outside the home. I'm not talking about external pressures. I'm talking about mommy guilt, exhaustion, second thoughts, and all those other self-doubts we layer upon ourselves. The battle that rages in one's own heart about what it means to be a Christian woman with a Kingdom assignment outside the family unit is a complex struggle. That internal conflict, along with the spiritual warfare that will come against you to get you off track, requires a battle-ready warrior response. Once you begin to understand that your work is your ministry to others, you can expect a battle to rage against your faith and against your purpose. The good news is you have every resource you need to be successful at your disposal. You are a warrior headed into battle, with an important Kingdom purpose that will allow you to uniquely impact the Kingdom of God. As you read your bible, pray without ceasing and seek the Lord's voice. You will find you are armed with strength for the important journey that lies ahead.

A warrior is a fierce, strong, brave, and skilled battle-ready fighter. A warrior fights the good fight and protects the weak and downtrodden. I can think of no greater purpose than to be assigned to impact the world in the place where most adults spend most of their time—in the marketplace. Seek your warrior purpose and put on your battle gear. An exciting and honorable assignment awaits.

REFLECTION

> **And who knows but that you have come to your royal position for such a time as this? (Esther 4:14)**

Reflect upon your own marketplace journey. Looking in the rearview mirror, you can probably see circumstances you encountered and choices you made that God ordained (or that He used) to get you closer to his Kingdom purpose. Take some time to think about how your life and calling fits into the Kingdom tapestry the Lord is weaving and how the childhood dreams and desires and your current marketplace assignment show His oversight and provision. Begin to focus on hearing God's voice and recognizing his influence upon your decision-making. Seeking him and recognizing the promptings and circumstances ordained by him will give you confidence as you discover your Kingdom purpose.

Take some time to consider the following, writing the answers down in a notebook set aside for this purpose:

- Do you believe God made you for ministry in the marketplace?
- Do you feel like God is proud of His creation in you?
- Are you using your talents for the service of others?
- Can you describe your godly warrior purpose?

- How can you improve on your obedience to God in the marketplace?
- Do you feel like God may have something else in store for you?
- Can you remember the earliest visions of God's plans for your life? If so, what were they?

HOMEWORK

- If your answer to any of the reflection questions is "no", make a note of these questions in your notebook so you can return to these later as the Lord reveals these things to you.
- Plan one way you'll increase your connection to God this week by seeking Him (e.g., listening to an audio bible teaching, reading a certain number of scripture verses or chapters every day, reading or listening to a daily devotional, etc.); write this down in your notebook as a reminder.

CHAPTER TWO:
GOD'S PLANS ARE PERFECT

Many are the plans in a person's heart, but it is the Lord's purpose that prevails. (Proverbs 19:21)

I was a stay-at-home mom with two kids and one on the way. Life took an awful turn, and I was going through a terrible divorce. I was limited in marketplace knowledge. I knew I needed formal education, so I went back to college and finished a psychology degree along with real estate courses. My plan was to continue on to graduate school, but I was not accepted into the course of study that I wanted. Disappointed but determined to support my family, I immediately launched into real estate. Since then I obtained my broker license in three states and started my own company. In this I have learned what I like to call "But God" moments. When I had a plan that didn't work out, I'd say, "But God"; when it was just too hard, "But God"; when my faith was low, "But God"; when there was no money coming in, "But God"; when I cried all night because I just couldn't do it, "But God"; when the burdens of single parenting were too big, "But God"; when there seemed to be no possible breakthrough, "But God"; when I wanted to give up, "But God". Those "But God" moments carried me one more minute to one more hour to one more day and another day and another day. Even when I wanted to give up, God did not give up on me. He ministered to me, and I in turn was able to make my life a ministry to others. He supplies for my needs, and in my weakness He used me to further His Kingdom.

—Jackie S.

WE READ IN GENESIS 17 THAT THE LORD appeared to Abram when he was ninety-nine years old. Ponder that for a moment. At 99, Abram was likely tired, having lived a lifetime fighting the good fight. We can imagine he was winding down his life and thinking about retirement. Instead, God appeared to him and told Abram if he would walk blamelessly, the Lord would make him the father of all nations. The Lord promised Abram a child. At 99. Father to all nations, and he doesn't even hear about this Kingdom purpose until he's 99. It wasn't too late for Abram, and it's not too late for you! It's never too late to hear from God, identify your Kingdom purpose, and walk out your Godly assignment. Until you take your last breath on this earth, your purpose is reserved only for you, and it is never too late to fulfill it. God's plans are perfect, and he will fulfill them in you.

At the age of twenty-nine (my husband was thirty-four), and while in the middle of a successful career in nursing (and my husband in clinical pharmacy), I had a great deal of unrest. I had strayed from the Lord of my youth and made some bad, immature decisions, and in my spirit I knew I was headed in the wrong direction. One day, in a wave of courage (or perhaps despair), I approached my husband to express my uneasiness at the path our lives seemed to be on. We had one young child at the time, and by the world's standards, from a financial and professional perspective, we had it all. We had a beautiful family; we had great jobs; we lived in a historic home in a big city, traveled as we desired, and owned all the newest electronics and toys.

Unfortunately we were disconnected as a family and as a couple, and we were running on what felt like a purposeless treadmill. By the grace of God we agreed to take the next eighteen months to plan and make huge life changes. God blessed these eighteen months as only He can, with provision and godly intervention all along the way (although we wouldn't recognize His presence or give Him the credit until years later). We put our home on the market and it sold in a matter of days. My husband found an entry-level job in a new profession that would spur him into a new successful career. I was accepted into law school many states away. We gave birth to our second child to complete our family before transitioning our lives, and we found the perfect farmhouse to rent in our new town to begin our new lives. We sold nearly everything we owned in order to save on moving expenses. We thought we were taking a giant leap of faith. Again, the rearview mirror clearly showed us years later that God fully ordained this important life change, as our "leap" was the beginning of us returning to the Lord, returning to each other, and ensuring we were fulfilling our God-given purposes for our marriage, our family, and our careers.

> **Do not be anxious about anything, but in every situation, by prayer and petition, with thanksgiving, present your requests to God. (Philippians 4:6)**

The world thought we were crazy. Give up good jobs? Give up a stable home to move halfway across the country and rent an old, weary farm house and go to law school at the age of thirty? Why would my husband start a new career at the entry level when he was at the top of his current industry? When you know your purpose and you seek to fulfill it with all your heart, God will honor your drive and your direction, and He will sustain you. He'll defy the wisdom of the world with His own. He will provide.

It would take us many years to fully understand God's plans for our family. We embarked on that long road that included law school, followed by several state-by-state moves as Jim's new career (not surprisingly) exploded with success and promotions. We found a church family and became active in our community; we began to raise our children in the church; we connected to godly people who would mentor and influence our path in a godly way; we met neighbors who introduced us to the importance of frequent fellowship with other believers; we grew in our knowledge of God. It all began by taking that giant leap of faith.

Only God knows the tapestry He's weaving. We're too close to the thread to see the big picture, but godly direction plus human obedience is a great and powerful combination. Don't be alarmed if you don't yet know all the chapters He's writing regarding His purpose for your life. If you believe God is directing you to make a move, *and that move lines up with the Word of God*, then He may be asking you to step out in faith and weave that one single thread. He'll give you what you need to know, as you need to know it, so long as you continue to keep your eyes upon Him.

You can't wander farther than the Father's arms can reach. He can use any mistake, any circumstance, and wrong turn in your life for the good of those who love Him. God is a kind and loving God who created you for an important role. Come to Him with a humble heart and repent of your sins. He will make your paths straight. It's never too late to seek His purpose for your life and to follow Him in obedience and faith.

My sheep listen to my voice; I know them, and they follow me. (John 10:6)

If you are genuinely seeking God's purpose for your life, you need to spend time in prayer asking Him what He created you for. If you are like I was, your life of busyness has resulted in you moving quiet time to the bottom of your priority list.

I urge you to move that back to the top. If you drive to work, buy yourself a bible on CD, download a favorite preacher's sermons on your iPod, and get daily devotionals delivered to your email inbox. Make an intentional effort to hear from God. Cry out to Him. When we seek Him, He does not hide himself from us. Learn to pray without ceasing, and listen for the prompting of the Holy Spirit within you.

I've met a lot of women who I am convinced find comfort in the angst; these are women who read every self-help book except the bible, and ask everyone except God what they should do with their lives. Angst isn't going to dissipate on its own, nor will your unrest settle down, until you seek the only direction and confirmation that matters, found only in the presence and direction of God. You can certainly make life changes without hearing from God, and you may even find temporary gain, but only those steps ordained by God bring lasting and persistent peace. Seek Him and you'll find Him every single time.

Just as a busy life clouds our ability (or willingness) to hear God, our overindulgence and abundance can have the same effect. I've found that integrating a fasting lifestyle into my spiritual journey allows me to schedule times each week to focus specifically and solely on hearing the shepherd's voice. Our church shares a twenty-one-day corporate fast at the beginning of each calendar year, and throughout the year I fast one twenty-four-hour period each week. The scheduled fast reminds me to be intentional about filling up on the things of God during that period; during this time, I only listen to sermons or Christian music, for example, instead of the national news or talk radio. One associate shared with me that she witnessed some of my best business decisions during these fasting periods. God is so good! If your medical condition allows it, and your doctor approves it, you may want to ask your church pastor about fasting, or seek a good online resource that will point you to the biblical foundation for seeking the Lord from a place of hunger.

> **As Jesus and his disciples were on their way, he came to a village where a woman named Martha opened her home to him. She had a sister called Mary, who sat at the Lord's feet listening to what he said. But Martha was distracted by all the preparations that had to be made. She came to him and asked, "Lord, don't you care that my sister has left me to do the work by myself? Tell her to help me!"**
>
> **"Martha, Martha," the Lord answered, "you are worried and upset about many things, but few things are needed—or**

indeed only one. Mary has chosen what is better, and it will not be taken away from her." (Luke 10:38–42)

I bet you can relate to Martha and wish you were more like Mary. Martha was wired like most working women, and if she were alive today, I think she'd be in line for a Fortune 500 CEO position. I've done several Martha/Mary bible studies and I find I always end up feeling a bit of secret pride that I'm like Martha. And then I get convicted, because that's not the point. God isn't interested in us having clean floors and dishes if we miss His presence in our home. It's not what God has called us to be. When we're overwhelmed and feeling like the pressure of all the responsibility we have is more than we can take, we're either on the verge of a breakdown or a breakthrough, but we're certainly not where God intends us to be in the craziness! As wives, mothers, businesswomen, and all of the many other hats we wear, we have a tendency to pile more onto our plates than any human being could possibly carry with any real measure of success.

In order to work through the list of responsibilities on your plate while asking God to reveal your purpose, you will be required to take an honest inventory of what drives you and what you're trying to accomplish with your heavy load. Let's call this exercise your "busy inventory". Before you heap more guilt onto your plate, remember that God loved *both*

Mary and Martha (John 11:5). God created you, so He understands your struggle to do it all. I can't stress enough that God's purpose for every single life is always a Kingdom purpose! Match up your to-do list with the reason you feel led to do each thing. Then ask yourself and God if there is a Kingdom purpose for each item. It's easy to see being a dedicated, devoted wife or a loving, caring mom as godly purposes. But why are you working twelve-hour days at the office? Perhaps you're in a job you just don't like, one that causes you stress and makes you miss soccer games and feel tremendous guilt. It's also possible you're in a job you love, yet you're feeling those exact same emotions. Only God can identify to your spirit your calling and His purpose and where you need to make changes.

I have had huge corporate marketplace positions that required me to spend many, many hours at the office and days on the road. Every Holy Spirit check that I did helped me to tweak my schedule and ensure that this continued to be God's purpose for my life. "It's all about salvation" is what the Lord frequently reminded me. He placed me in secular companies, in executive positions where I would boldly proclaim the gospel and the love of Christ. Souls were saved. By modeling a servant leadership style, I was able to share the love of Christ from the smallest of interactions to the most complex. Business boomed and succeeded in a manner that defied man's business sense. My godly assignment is to be obedient to the Lord placing me "in the chair" where He expects me to perform in the workplace in a manner different from the ways of the world, for the purpose of expanding the Kingdom. God in turn honors that obedience with prophetic impartation of business strategies and ordaining business success. When I grow weary from long days and high pressure, I sit down in prayer and write my "Busy List". I ensure I am focused on the things the Lord has called me to do and that I haven't taken on Martha's superhuman desire to do it all. I then clean up my list and let go of the things that I don't believe are part of my Kingdom purpose. I remember that God created the assignment and that He is in the planning and execution of the assignment, no matter how big or how small. He expects only my best, nothing more. My stress doesn't further his purpose nor does it keep me equipped to stay in the chair.

If you are in a job that feels less than optimal, and you're there because you're supporting your family, don't discount that as a very honorable Kingdom purpose in itself. My prayer for you is supernatural strength and stamina, and may you do your work as if unto the Lord. May you be surrounded with supportive friends, and may you shine the light as you grow where you are planted. I urge you to look at that position with fresh eyes. If God is thriving your family with this job, what are you doing to act with integrity, inspire excellence, and positively impact others as you walk out this season of your life? Are you being called to make a change, or are you called to grow your ministry where you are planted? Seek the Lord's direction in all you do. He knows the plans He has for you. (Jeremiah 29:11)

You may believe you have good reasons to change jobs or to even seek a new profession. While that may be okay to explore (that's a decision between you, your family, and God), remember that all jobs and all workplaces are mission fields. Be less concerned with finding the perfect job and more focused on turning your work into your ministry. God doesn't consider one profession godlier than another. Grow where you are planted. Seek God's direction. Look for His presence in opportunities that are around you. Peace is a great barometer of being smack dab in the middle of God's will for your life. Mary was at peace sitting at the feet of Jesus, while Martha was stressed trying to get everything done.

Likewise, if your family will eat just fine without you in the job that is causing you great stress, and you can't find your purpose anywhere in it, then you need to do some soul searching. I can't express to you enough that God created you for a specific purpose. Perhaps you need to get on a different path. Only the Lord can give you peace concerning your next move. This is your opportunity to dive back into your quiet time with the Lord, search His word, spend serious time in prayer, and wait to hear His voice.

Here's a newsflash: It's okay to leave a job if that's what the Lord is calling you to do! It's okay to take a break and stay home for a year or two to be with your babies if your family economics allow, your heart desires, and the Holy Spirit leads you to! Life might be better for you if you don't have the big fancy title and the big car! In my thirty-plus years mentoring women in the workplace, I've had the honor of encouraging and teaching many to raise their hands and voices in order to be heard over the men and to be promoted. I've also challenged women to discern if they are really doing what they were created and meant to do, and if they aren't, to dare to enroll in school, take a step down the ladder to take a step up a different ladder, or leave a company altogether to get to their right purpose. God's purpose is God's purpose. You can be on a good path or a successful path, but it *still* could be the *wrong* path. So don't be afraid to let go of success to make a change. I can tell you from experience there is no greater satisfaction than obedience that allows you to jump from the wrong road to the right one!

> **It does not, therefore, depend on human desire or effort, but on God's mercy. For Scripture says to Pharaoh: "I raised you up for this very purpose,**

that I might display my power in you and that my name might be proclaimed in all the earth." Therefore God has mercy on whom he wants to have mercy, and he hardens whom he wants to harden. (Romans 9:16–18)

This summer I had a beautiful handmade wreath on our front door of our home. It was apparently quite inviting because in short order a momma bird made a nest and laid her eggs in the middle of my beautiful wreath before I could intervene and help her find a better way. Our family made an effort for the next several days and weeks to carefully open and shut the door so as to create as little disruption as possible for the mother and her plan for her little ones. We watched as the eggs hatched; we even started using a different entrance to our home so as to not interrupt when the mother bird was feverishly working to feed them with humans too close for her comfort.

One day Jim walked by the wreath and saw one of the poor young birds on the floor. These babies had become precious to us, and the mother's persistent care of her young had earned our highest respect. My husband gently picked up the baby and very carefully placed him back in the nest. That day, three additional times, Jim found one or more of those babies out of the nest, sitting under the wreath on the floor. Each time he carefully and gently replaced them in the nest. Later that same day, from the quiet of our window, we saw the mother pushing her babies with her beak out of the nest, making them fall to the floor. The mother was working feverishly to get those babies outside their comfort zone and off to fulfill their purpose—to fly into the wild and leave that precariously positioned nest in the beautiful wreath where they were warm and comfortable. Little did we know we were intervening by applying our interpretation of the situation and offering rescue when in fact our "rescue" hindered their growth and development. We needed to get out of the mother bird's way and allow her to push her babies outside their comfort zone. Only then would they spread their wings and learn to fly.

Of this I am certain: Fulfilling your purpose will require you to grow, and growth only happens outside the comfort zone. Dare to leave your nest of comfort as you begin to walk out your workplace assignment as ministry—then fly! Don't be surprised if someone tries to put you back where they think you belong a time or two or even three.

REFLECTION

> **Now to each one the manifestation of the Spirit is given for the common good. (1 Corinthians 12)**

- How has God revealed His purpose to you?
- How do you see God revealing your professional calling?
- How can you increase your ministry impact at the workplace (e.g., through encouraging people or having a servant heart)?
- Is God calling you to take a leap of faith?

HOMEWORK

- Read and journal your thoughts on the story of Martha and Mary in Luke 10.
- Complete your "Busy List" with three columns, identifying each task, why you do it, and its godly purpose.
- Ask yourself: Is God calling you to reprioritize your list?
- Write down in your notebook one new way you'll continue to increase your connection to God this week by seeking Him.

CHAPTER THREE:
RECONCILING THE PROVERBS 31 WOMAN

She is worth far more than rubies. Her husband has full confidence in her and lacks nothing of value. She brings him good, not harm, all the days of her life. She selects wool and flax and works with eager hands. She is like the merchant ships, bringing her food from afar. She gets up while it is still night; she provides food for her family and portions for her female servants. She considers a field and buys it; out of her earnings she plants a vineyard. She sets about her work vigorously; her arms are strong for her tasks. She sees that her trading is profitable, and her lamp does not go out at night. In her hand she holds the distaff and grasps the spindle with her fingers. (Proverbs 31:10–19)

Two years ago, the Lord sent me on a women's ministry retreat with four of my Christian friends. At that time I was supporting my pastor husband with my gifts and talents. I felt like the Lord was calling me to a new season—and new chapter—to enter the marketplace to impact the Kingdom. Leaving church ministry to step into business was a step of faith most certainly and way outside my comfort zone. More importantly, it was obedience to the Lord's calling, even when I didn't know what the next step would lead to or what the Lord had in mind. Today, by faith, walking in response to His call has allowed me to impact hundreds, perhaps even thousands, by providing care and compassion to those in the business world. In my travels, the Lord positions me in the right place at the right time. All I have to do is be available to those in need.

—Karen S.

Perhaps you groaned when you saw the chapter title, thinking, *oh, no—not another lecture on how to be a good Proverbs 31 wife!* If you feel that way, please allow me to say this: On behalf of the many well-meaning church ladies who have told you God intends for you to stay home and work your "farm", I'm sorry. Consider this instead: God inspired this passage for women exactly like us. The woman described here is certainly a working woman—*and* a warrior. She has tremendous influence in the life of her husband and her family. She works tirelessly; she's responsible and strong and wise; she honors God in all she does; she's a worker, a doer, an independent thinker, and a leader.

The Proverbs 31 wife is an intelligent, responsible, intuitive, caring, talented woman who manages her homestead and has money to invest at the end of the day. She is her husband's partner and a strong force to be reckoned with by any account. Through the Proverbs 31 woman, the Lord is giving us an important mental picture to emulate as godly women, regardless of where our Kingdom assignment places us. God can call you to honor your husband, fulfill your responsibilities to your family, and love your work, all at the same time.

I remember one particular Thursday evening many years ago, feeling despondent as I sat in a church pew following choir rehearsal. I held an executive position at the corporate headquarters of that growing healthcare management company that was based in downtown Chicago. Work pressures were already mounting. My sixty-mile suburban commute to Michigan Avenue was long and difficult—hours by car, and a less than desirable train schedule didn't make public transportation a better alternative. Our suburban home was expensive (as all Chicago homes are) and private school bills were a heavy load.

We had finally connected with a great church and were learning to live by the principles of Jesus Christ. Worship was my passion, and I loved the opportunity to join the choir. It was the creative outlet I desired, but it took even more precious time away from my family. This particular night I was overflowing with mommy guilt and feeling completely overwhelmed. My fellow choir mates, a wonderful group of God-fearing women, surrounded me to comfort me with one resoundingly simple message. "Quit your job. God intends for you to be in the home, especially with small children and a hard-working husband. Be a Proverbs 31 wife after all." BAM! My guilt plate overflowed. God had brought us so far, and even though I was having a bad day, I believed in my gut that I was walking out my godly purpose in my new job. Certainly this professional opportunity was God positioning me for His bigger plans. But boy did I feel guilty about the time commitments away from my family and my husband and my home.

Surely God knew of this struggle, didn't He? Saddled with the guilt enhanced by the words of my choir mates, I cried to my husband that night, and after much discussion, we agreed that the time away from our home (and especially our girls) was just too much. I was crumbling under the pressure of the new role; a weight compounded by the exhausting commute.

The very next day I took the train into my office in Chicago and told my boss I was sorry, but I had to resign. While I loved the new executive role, and was excited about the professional opportunity, I had to put my family first. The extraordinary commute and long hours were more than I could balance. I couldn't have it all. It was a Friday, and my boss told me she was sad to hear my news, but she understood. She asked me to give it additional thought over the weekend and to not consider my resignation final until we met again on Monday. I told her I would do that, but I didn't believe I'd change my mind.

> **"For I know the plans I have for you," declares the LORD, "plans to prosper you and not to harm you, plans to give you hope and a future." (Jeremiah 29:11)**

I left the office that Friday evening discouraged and feeling like a failure in all things. Running to the train station to catch the last train out to the suburbs, I was sweaty, tired, and angry. I wouldn't call my conversation with God during that race to the train quite prayerful or thankful. I jumped onto my usual train car to find the air conditioning broken and only one remaining unoccupied seat. I hurried to the seat before someone else took it. Lying on the seat was a picture a little bigger than a business card. I picked up the picture before plopping down in the seat. It was a picture of the face of Jesus Christ wearing a bloody crown of thorns. On it was a message: "For I know the plans I have for you..."

I began to weep. This would serve as a memorable time in my adult life when I would recognize *how much God loves me*. He knew how difficult I found my assignment. Perhaps He was trying to tell me He would keep me in the palm of His hand every step of the way, if only I would rely upon Him. With this in mind, I tucked the picture in my pocket, wiped my nose and dried my tears. In the midst of my disappointment in my circumstances, the Creator of the Universe was comforting me and I felt a spark of peace. Surely it would all work out as it should.

That weekend, my husband and I reflected on the situation further. We still couldn't figure out how to make the time commitment of the long commute work for our family, so we didn't change our decision that I would resign. The fourteen-hour days away from my family were just too much. I returned to the office the following Monday, comfortable that God was in this decision. Wherever He took me next would be okay.

My boss called me into her office. "We don't want you to leave," she said. "We'd like to get creative. Would it work better for you if you did your job from your home?"

Wow. As He would time and time and time again, God came through in an amazing way. He not only gave me the assignment that required what I thought was super human strength and stamina like I always thought the Proverbs 31 woman had, God himself provided all the strength and stamina required to fulfill his Kingdom purpose. A work-from-home schedule eliminated every single stressor that came with the position. With this development, I was back on track and on my way to fulfilling my godly purpose in the marketplace. For the next seven years, the Lord used that professional position to teach, train, and grow me. He broadened my knowledge, my assignment, and my purpose, and set me on the course for even bigger and better things.

> **When the whole nation had finished crossing the Jordan, the Lord said to Joshua, "Choose twelve men from among the people, one from each tribe, and tell them to take up twelve**

stones from the middle of the Jordan, from right where the priests are standing, and carry them over with you and put them down at the place where you stay tonight."

So Joshua called together the twelve men he had appointed from the Israelites, one from each tribe, and said to them, "Go over before the ark of the Lord your God into the middle of the Jordan. Each of you is to take up a stone on his shoulder, according to the number of the tribes of the Israelites, to serve as a sign among you. In the future, when your children ask you, 'What do these stones mean?' tell them that the flow of the Jordan was cut off before the ark of the covenant of the Lord. When it crossed the Jordan, the waters of the Jordan were cut off. These stones are to be a memorial to the people of Israel forever." (Joshua 4: 1–7)

God's provision in that Chicago job is just one example of how God can—and will—part the Jordan River for you and me. The bible is full of examples of His love and provision as He comes through at just the right time to deliver, provide, and intervene. He parted the Jordan River for Joshua and the Israelites. Joshua was faithful to follow God's lead, and God provided. He gave the Proverbs 31 woman all the strength, stamina, and wisdom she needed to fulfill her Kingdom purpose. He did the same for me. As we fulfill God's Kingdom purpose, he'll be there to provide exactly what we need, when we need it. He is a faithful God setting us up for success, partnering with us as we seek his direction. I love the next part of Joshua's story, too. Not only did the Lord part the river, but he also instructed Joshua to teach the people how to remember all that God had done, by picking up a rock. I don't want to forget all the Lord has done for me either, and picking up rocks is a habit I've adopted from Joshua's example.

From that commuter train I picked up a "rock" and placed it in my pocket. That picture of Jesus Christ that someone laid on the train seat (as part of their own ministry, I suppose) still sits, now framed, on my desk in my home office today. And for many, many years, when I've had moments when life seems impossibly complicated, it has served as a reminder to take a step back and remember to give it all up to Him. He gave the assignment; he knows what it requires to get it done. Put God first in your planning of how to accomplish all you believe you've been called to do. It's way too overwhelming to figure out how to fulfill all your responsibilities as a Proverbs 31 woman on your own strength. Rely on God to guide you, and He'll work out the details at the precise time you need them worked out. Remember, we serve a God who never abandons us in our time of need. Wait for him. He fulfills His plan perfectly in His own time.

> **"A woman who fears the Lord will not run away from God to satisfy her longings and relieve her anxieties. She will wait for the Lord. She will hope in God. She will stay close to the heart of God and trust in his promises. The prospect of departing into the way of sin will be too fearful to pursue; and the benefits of abiding in the shadow of the Almighty too glorious to forsake." Pastor John Piper, 1981 Mother's Day Sermon**

God has called you to live out your ministry in the marketplace. Trust that he will provide all you need as you wait upon Him; trust in Him, abiding in the shadow of his wings. He'll provide for you in surprising ways, just as He did for Joshua. Be certain to pick up "rocks" along the way to remind yourself how good the Lord has been to you. I never want to get to a place that I think my success is related to my own brilliance and capabilities. Rather, I remember my successes depend upon using the gifts He's given me, under His guidance and direction, to serve His Kingdom and His purpose alone. Keep a journal; pick up tokens; do something to remind yourself, as you walk out your godly purpose, that the creator of the universe is clearing the way; guiding, watching, and protecting you.

God made you just the way you are, including all the attributes you see as flaws and those pesky personality traits that sometimes get in your way. He knows your assignment feels big and difficult and sometimes even daunting. There's nothing to reconcile here. Proverbs 31 describes you perfectly—He knew that, too. God doesn't tell us to be superwomen—those passages describe a woman firmly leaning upon the Lord to accomplish incredible feats. Lean on Him; He'll provide you numerous opportunities to see His hand at work in your assignment and success.

REFLECTION

> **But God is my helper. The Lord keeps me alive! (Psalm 54:4)**

God had you in mind when he gave us the description in Proverbs 31.

- Read the Proverbs 31 passage again. Do you feel like this describes you?
- Do all of the verses describe you? If not, which ones do not? Which ones do?
- Are you comfortable with the idea that a woman who works outside her home can meet the biblical description of a godly wife?
- Do you fear the Lord like the woman described in this passage?

HOMEWORK

- Make a list in your journal of your "Joshua rocks"—times when God so clearly intervened in your life in a way you'll never forget.
- Are there areas where you feel like you're letting God down when you reflect upon Proverbs 31? Write these thoughts in your journal, and pray for God's provision and guidance and that you'll recognize your strength comes from the Lord.
- Continue to seek Him in prayer and in reading His Word. Write your plan for the week in your journal.

CHAPTER FOUR:
LOVING ZACCHAEUS

Jesus entered Jericho and was passing through. A man was there by the name of Zacchaeus; he was a chief tax collector and was wealthy. He wanted to see who Jesus was, but because he was short he could not see over the crowd. So he ran ahead and climbed a sycamore-fig tree to see him, since Jesus was coming that way.

When Jesus reached the spot, he looked up and said to him, "Zacchaeus, come down immediately. I must stay at your house today." So he came down at once and welcomed him gladly. All the people saw this and began to mutter, "He has gone to be the guest of a sinner." But Zacchaeus stood up and said to the Lord, "Look, Lord! Here and now I give half of my possessions to the poor, and if I have cheated anybody out of anything, I will pay back four times the amount." Jesus said to him, "Today salvation has come to this house..." (Luke 19: 1–9)

God didn't just call you to grow an organization—he qualified you to transform hearts. It is because of your perseverance, hope, and love for the lost that you never gave up on me, even when I gave up on myself, that I learned what it really means to be a child of God. The workplace is often the toughest place to walk in faith. For me, it's where I was taught that through Christ, all things really are possible.

—*Christina S.*

But for the love of Jesus Christ, we're all like Zacchaeus, just the short guy in the tree curious about what's going on, lost and in need of a better perspective. We are positioned *in* the world, called *to love* the world, but not *of* the world. Christ died on the cross presenting a perfect and complete sacrifice for our sins. For those of us who believe, repent of our sins, and ask Jesus Christ to be our Lord and Savior, there is everlasting life. We are commanded as believers to love others as Christ first loved us. Christ died for us. That's how much He loved us while we were lost and wretched sinners. He's calling us to love the lost as well.

The executive position I held in Chicago required occasional state-to-state travel, which was a new experience for me. I left my family for my first-ever work-related trip and headed to Providence, Rhode Island to gather my regional team for a planning session. The date was September 10, 2001. I'd flown only once or twice previously in my entire life and had never left my family overnight, so I was already reflecting on the magnitude of this new responsibility with a newfound trust that God would provide.

Once I was on the plane, I took my place at the window seat. There was a woman in the seat closest to the aisle; she looked like a businesswoman who was also on a travel assignment. We nodded at each other but didn't speak. Soon a young man who appeared to be in his early twenties or thereabouts—and who also appeared to be of Middle Eastern descent—took the seat between us. From the moment he sat down, he was shaking uncontrollably. His knees jerked up and down nonstop, and he was sweating profusely. I exchanged glances with the woman in the aisle seat, and I could tell she was as uncomfortable with his behavior as I was. Clearly he was struggling with something that weighed heavily on his mind. The tension in our row was palpable. I thanked God as we landed in Providence, glad to be exiting the plane. Still shaken, I immediately found a payphone and called my husband. What on earth was I doing this far away from my family, flying with a crazy person instead of at home reading bedtime stories to my girls?

The next morning, September 11, 2001, delivered the biggest US tragedy in modern history as terrorists flew planes into the World Trade Center and the Pentagon. We watched the horror unfold from our meeting place in Providence. When I returned to my hotel that afternoon, the streets of Providence outside my hotel and around the Amtrak station across the street were filled with armed police and guards. I wondered at that moment if my seat-mate was somehow related to the terrorist activity and if I had been sitting only inches from evil. I phoned the FBI as the media had requested and reported my flight and seat numbers, along with a description of the anxious young man next to me. And in the ensuing days that followed, I, along with millions of other Americans, spent time searching for all that was good and right in this world.

I spent a lot of time thinking about my godly purpose as I left Rhode Island and drove my rental car toward Chicago. My husband left Chicago with the girls and drove in my direction as we agreed to meet wherever we could in the middle. *Life is fragile; shouldn't I be at home with my family?* I thought. In the hours I spent driving, I had an overwhelming understanding that the world is a lost and fallen place and that the battlefield is keenly spiritual. It became clear to me that if people of faith hide their light beneath a rock, nothing will change. I felt God calling me even more fervently into the marketplace—not for my own gain, but for ministry. As a missionary of sorts, I would play some small role for the Kingdom to bring His light into the darkness.

The example of the interaction between Jesus and Zacchaeus is relevant to us today. Zacchaeus was a tax collector; a profession of the time that involved fraud and cheating. No one liked Zacchaeus, but this unlikely subject was chosen by Christ, and forever changed by his interaction with Christ. Jesus chose someone who the world said wasn't worthy to be chosen. Jesus loved Zacchaeus with his actions and his words. He gave Zacchaeus the simple gift of time to share a meal. Zacchaeus was converted and became a zealous follower of Christ.

We're living in a lost and broken world. And yes, the world is a dangerous place. As marketplace ministers, we have a unique opportunity to reach the lost and the unloved. Most adults spend more time in the workplace than they spend any other place other than sleeping. Our ministry doesn't even require us to find hurting folks up in trees. They're everywhere around us. Imagine the impact and the magnitude of a ministry that meets people where they are and where they least expect to be loved and cared for. Being called to ministry in the workplace is perhaps the highest calling of all.

> **Because he was a tentmaker as they were, he stayed and worked with them. (Acts 18:3)**

Have you ever thought of Paul as a marketplace minister? He was, after all, a tentmaker. We don't know if he put his tent-making aside to preach the gospel, but we have at least this example of him working beside those he preached to. I believe we don't have this clear understanding because Paul didn't bifurcate his life. He didn't have a preaching life and a separate tent-making life. Paul's life was his ministry, just as all Christians' lives are called to be, regardless of how we spend the hours in our day. Think of all the people you interact with every single day in your work environment who don't know the Lord. It's exciting to think about the Kingdom impact you can have just by being like Christ as you do your tent-making or whatever profession you're carrying out.

I hope you're beginning to think of your work as your life's ministry. A marketplace purpose is a special calling. I believe women are making a huge impact on the corporate culture of many businesses today as we lead from the front with a servant leadership style, able to handle the most complex of business strategies while nurturing and growing those we lead. If those of us who are believers also begin to live out our purpose as ministry, I believe we'll find our own satisfaction, *as well as the fruits of our labor,* increase as a result.

Up to this point in your life, you may have known you desired to be successful in your work but kept that part of your brain separate from your "home self", the wife, mother, go-to-church-on-Sunday self. That's one of the reasons we run ourselves so ragged. That dual personality takes a lot of effort and time. You have one personality, one mind, one set of emotions—and one purpose. Stop putting your work down and picking up your home life; stop putting your home life down and picking up your work life. Stop thinking of your life as a balancing act. Rather, start thinking about a *blended* life, where ministry is your life's purpose.

As strong, intelligent, marketplace-minded women, the same leading and prompting that we are keenly aware of in our prayer and spiritual life is available to us in our workplace. Learn to hone and listen to this Holy Spirit prompting or "intuition" in order to author and execute creative, successful business ideas. Seek the Lord's guidance and direction in everything, not just "big" business decisions. God wants you to impact the Kingdom. He'll give you all the tools you need to make a big impact if you ask and listen.

With an electronic bible always available in my car's CD player, I have the opportunity to begin my day listening to the Word of God, no matter what my schedule looks like. I also keep favorite sermons downloaded on my smartphone and keep teaching CDs as "spiritual food", which all help me to be intentional in my desire to live out my ministry. Sticky notes are my friends; it's not uncommon for me to have scripture or keywords (like "pray" or "warrior") posted on my keyboard or monitor to remind me I'm in ministry. I talk to the Lord throughout the day.

One technique you might employ is to ask the Lord what He thinks of each person as you walk through aisles of cubicles or even as you sit across from a person in a meeting. The occasional prompting of the Holy Spirit is an incredibly powerful thing, and the bible says when we seek Him, He does not hide himself from His flock. The Lord, from time to time, gives me impressions of pain or sorrow or joy and sometimes even a discernment of darkness in people. I am then able to privately and in a very personal way send up appropriate prayers for the person or situation. Praying without ceasing is key to marketplace ministry, and it is easier than you might think. It's really just constantly talking to God in your head. No matter what you're doing, just have a conversation with God about it. When you practice it, prayer becomes muscle memory.

I remember one particular event when I was working as a bedside nurse in a critical care unit. I would consider the bedside of a critically ill patient an "easy" place to think of oneself as a "minister". This particular patient was a known drug dealer and Satan worshipper in our small town. I was assigned to be his primary caregiver and his condition from a drug overdose was extremely dire. He was in a coma. While working over him, adjusting tubes and machinery, the Holy Spirit quickly prodded me to pray vigorously without ceasing. So I did. I prayed out loud as I cared for him for whatever the spirit brought to mind, for healing, forgiveness, knowledge of God, repentance. I sang worship songs and prayed some more for hours on end. This gentleman died late that same day. I have no idea what impact to the Kingdom my obedience had (it's on my list to ask Jesus one day), but I know it had one. Perhaps the prayer and worship protected me in the face of evil, or perhaps in his coma state he accepted Christ. It's not for me to know. I loved the sinner in the tree as the Holy Spirit commanded me to do. Some professions might seem more geared to ministry (like nursing), but I'm challenging you to see that every workplace is in need of your faithfulness to your Kingdom calling.

> **For God does speak—now one way, now another—though no one perceives it. In a dream, in a vision of the night, when deep sleep falls on people as they slumber in their beds, he may speak in their ears and terrify them with warnings, to turn them from wrongdoing and keep them from pride. (Job 33:17)**

I listen carefully to thoughts that enter my mind that seem to come out of nowhere or that seem to be unrelated or to make no sense. In my experience, those thoughts often end up being pure "God-genius" and result in significant business success (and I can say that without boasting because they were the Lord's successes, not mine). Many times, the Holy Spirit is prompting me to guide and bless the lost, all for a Kingdom purpose.

These instances of "God-genius" can happen without warning, so you'll really want to always be ready to receive direction from the Lord. Sometimes it will be easy to discern and won't take much for you to interpret and act upon. One such time I was interviewing a young gentleman for a position. He was quite qualified and experienced for the role. As he was speaking, a crazy thought entered my mind. Instead of hiring him for this position, my thoughts said he was in fact the person who would successfully fill a completely different role in another department (a position that was not yet vacant). After prayer and contemplation, I was convinced this was indeed the prompting of the Holy Spirit, and I positioned this person for that unintended role. He not only served successfully there, he made a significant impact and was promoted several times.

Sometimes the Holy Spirit will prompt you to make a move that's not quite so simple to effectuate. One example of this I cling to as it reminds me that obedience results in great blessings, and we may never know what we missed out on if we don't listen and act as we're called to do. I met with a gentleman who was in charge of a competitor business to discuss collaboration in a market that the company I worked for was entering. I didn't know this man and had identified his name through competitive research. I asked a local acquaintance about the gentleman and was told only that it was unlikely he would agree to meet with me. I called the competitor to ask for a meeting, and as I had been warned, he was rude to me on the phone and told me we had nothing to talk about. Surprisingly, when I asked a second time, he agreed to a meeting. I met with him at the agreed-upon time at his place of business. He was curt and animated and, as I suspected, he wasn't interested in our company being in "his" town. I barely spoke a word for nearly an hour, and he seemed to enjoy every minute of the exercise. At the end of an hour, I stood to leave, feeling like the meeting had been a complete waste of my time.

When I went to shake his hand as I exited, a crazy thought came to my mind: *I should ask him if he homeschools his children.* My initial response to the crazy thought in my head was this: *There is no way this man* (who had been sprinkling profanity into our conversation) *homeschools his children!* My second thought was: *Is this you, Lord?* I had come to know that crazy thoughts and "coincidences" like this were often from the Lord. I suppose we could attribute my obedience that day to the fact that I had nothing to lose with this meeting, so while shaking his hand goodbye I asked, "By any chance do you homeschool your kids?"

I wish I had a picture of the expression on his face. The mention of his children immediately changed his demeanor and clearly my question was spot on.

"Why would you ask me that?" he asked.

I told him I wasn't sure, and I relayed to him my own nontraditional arrangement. At this point in our lives, Jim and I were juggling our careers with homeschooling our children.

We were fortunate to be part of a large church-based organization that offered parent-led instruction, and we were able to work while our children attended parent led co-ops and other church-based learning. As working parents, we were definitely unusual homeschool parents, but the arrangement worked for Jim and I and allowed us to raise our children as we believed we were called to do, while also pursuing careers.

As it turned out, not only did he and his wife homeschool their kids, but he was especially proud of his wife, a professional working woman who was also taking a nontraditional approach for her family. It was clear by the change in his demeanor that I had struck the one topic that softened this man: his family. He motioned that we should sit back down. We talked another hour about family and then we revisited our business conversation, where we fashioned the beginning of our collaboration. Our companies would go forward from that meeting to work together successfully for many years, forging a relationship that was key to the success of both of our businesses. I am convinced if I had ignored that voice in my head, our successful entry into that market would have taken a very different course. Obedience (listening and responding to the Lord's voice) ushered in a favorable business relationship. Many families were positively impacted, and the Kingdom was expanded as a result.

Sometimes your obedience will be solely for the purpose of highlighting God's presence and power over success. I was having lunch with a key investor early in a fiscal year. Making small talk, but genuinely interested, he asked me where I thought the company would end the year financially. I was careful not to trap myself into an answer that might be way off and reflect poorly on the team's performance if I projected wrong. It was, after all, way too early in the year to make *any* kind of declaration with any confidence. Out of nowhere, a number sounded in my head. The number was higher than any budget forecast; it was a number that frankly defied common sense. I felt strongly this was the prompting of the Holy Spirit, so defying my own common sense I said the number out loud. I am absolutely certain he thought I was crazy. I know I thought I was crazy to say the number out loud!

We ended that fiscal year—you guessed it—at *exactly* that budget-defying number to which I publicly *and often* gave all the credit to the Lord. Results that only the Lord could ordain, along with public proclamation of the Lord's favor, was a ministry offering to the lost. I know that seeds were planted and fertilized as the lost pondered the mystery of results such as these.

And sometimes, the Lord's goodness will benefit individuals in a very personal way. One day, a young woman came into my office to resign. She was stressed with her work and she and her husband were having difficulties getting pregnant.

Her doctor had told her to decrease the amount of stress in her life, so through tears she told me she needed to leave the organization. She was one of the company's best employees, and I didn't want her to leave. I had an overwhelming feeling to both help her and to pray over her. I had no idea if she was a believer, and this feeling wasn't what I usually felt when someone asked me to pray with them. It was almost urgent—as if I *had* to pray over her.

I told her we'd transfer her to a less stressful role if she was willing, then asked if I could pray for her; she agreed. I hugged her, and the Holy Spirit prayed a powerful prayer related to her calling and the calling of her children that would come. She sobbed in my arms. When I finished praying, she wiped away her tears. I told her I'd have a new position for her the next day, and she was grateful. A few weeks later, while she was on vacation, she sent me a message:

You're never going to believe it: I'm pregnant!

Of course, I thought. *God, you are so good!*

I have so many of these anecdotes that I couldn't tell them all to you here. Don't get me wrong: God isn't a lucky eight ball or a magic wand. He calls us to do our work as unto the Lord. If you are obedient, He will bless your business, others around you, individuals will come to know Christ, you will personally grow, and the Kingdom will advance as He continues to weave the tapestry. As a business leader, I am called to lead with integrity and to honor, mentor, serve, and minister to those around me. He also calls me to boldly proclaim my faith in, and dependence upon, the Lord. That is my marketplace calling and my purpose. So long as I am faithful to that calling, He will do the rest. He delivers business ideas, moves the hearts of competitors, brings great people around me, provides opportunities, and delivers successful results as only He can for one purpose: furthering His Kingdom. And I sit "in the chair" in awe and try to keep up with Him by being an obedient, hard-working, discerning vessel.

When you begin to look at your work as your ministry, I believe by its very nature you will consider it a higher calling than you do today. Whether you sit in a cubicle on the phone interacting with clients all day or lead a large organization, your ability to positively impact lives and encourage and lift people up will be more clearly understood when you look at each interaction as a holy assignment from the Lord. You need to find your rhythm in your ministry and discover how the Lord will speak to you and guide you.

As a believer placed in a secular marketplace, you are called to bring all the lessons of Jesus Christ with you. You can be successful and innovative and beat the competition by applying godly principles to your everyday practice. If you pray without ceasing and rely on God to provide your business ideas, you'll find, as I did, that He rewards obedience and will highlight to you those whose lives He's going to use you to impact positively. Some of these people will be believers. More will be those who don't know Jesus but rather will see Him through your actions, obedience, and provision. God shows up when we seek Him—every single time. The Holy Spirit's purpose is to guide us in all things. You've got the best and most innovative business coach living right inside you. God speaks. Listen up!

> **When he had finished washing their feet, he put on his clothes and returned to his place. "Do you understand what I have done for you?" he asked them. "You call me 'Teacher' and 'Lord,' and rightly so, for that is what I am. Now that I, your Lord and Teacher, have washed your feet, you also should wash one another's feet. I have set you an example that you should do as I have done for you. (John 13:12–15)**

You may wonder how to create a culture of care in your organization in a way that allows open prayer, bible study, or spiritual care when, in many cases, political correctness rules and people look for any opportunity to sue. There certainly isn't one blueprint that will work for all marketplace conditions. Some positions by their very nature will have more flexibility and freedom to be bold in your faith. Others will require you act out the ministry of Christ without the words. Living like Jesus—using your gifts and talents to serve others regardless of your business position—is always an effective way to live out ministry. I always remind myself that the creator of the universe, not any secular board of directors, has given me my Kingdom assignments in business. I walk in faith that He who called me to the ministry will protect me in turn with His mercy and grace.

When trials come—and they always do—you'll need to focus on trusting God, so pray without ceasing. I have found when you treat people around you with genuine care and love, regardless of their worldview or belief system, most will accept that care and love gladly. This is true especially in the marketplace because it's so unexpected. Let what will come, come.

There are hurting people everywhere; treat people the way you like to be treated—even when the world says that's a risky move. Set an example for others, just as Jesus did for us. Apply that concept to business decisions, hiring standards, contract negotiations, and financial discussions. You'll be blessed. Every employee wants to work for an organization that gives back, shares its resources, loves people, and cares for the greater good. Any role you play in advancing those goals will be rewarding.

REFLECTION

**We love because He first loved us.
(1 John 4:19)**

- How different might your work be if you made Jesus front and center in your business planning?
- What reminders can you put in your workspace to remind you that your work is ministry to others?
- Do you love the lost that are all around you?
- Do you think God can give you business ideas?
- How can you share the love of Christ in your everyday workplace?
- How can you be like Jesus and choose Zacchaeus from up in the tree?

HOMEWORK

- Make a list of "coincidences" or circumstances that connect you to lost people in the workplace, and in hindsight seem like they must have been from God. Is there a way you can be on the lookout for these as they happen?
- How do you "hear" the Shepherd's voice?
- Think about ways you can show the love of Christ to the lost from a practical perspective. Write these in your notebook.
- Plan one way you'll increase your connection to God this week by seeking Him. Reflect on what and how you did last week, and write your assessment in your journal.

CHAPTER FIVE:
PUT ON YOUR LISTENING EARS

Don't waste what is holy on people who are unholy. Don't throw your pearls to pigs! They will trample the pearls, then turn and attack you. (Matthew 7:6)

...For all have sinned and fall short of the glory of God, and all are justified freely by his grace through the redemption that came by Christ Jesus. God presented Christ as a sacrifice of atonement through the shedding of his blood—to be received by faith. He did this to demonstrate his righteousness, because in his forbearance he had left the sins committed beforehand unpunished—he did it to demonstrate his righteousness at the present time, so as to be just and the one who justifies those who have faith in Jesus. (Romans 3:23-26)

The knowledge of the Kingdom of God needs to be in every aspect of my life. I refuse to shut it off when the people around me don't yet know Him. In fact, I believe by faith that I play a part in them becoming a child of God.

—Laurie D.

As a Christian woman in the marketplace, I am confident of two things. First, God will place you in the midst of numerous people who need your kindness and who need to know Christ and his gift of salvation. Second, when you're successfully reflecting Christ to others, forces will come against you to prevent your success. Unwittingly, there are those around you who will seek to trip up your purpose. You must always have your discernment game face on. Don't get off track by throwing pearls at swine.

In the secular marketplace, you are uniquely situated to witness and love people who need to know Jesus Christ each and every day. You have been given the unique opportunity in the workplace to impact people for the Kingdom; they may have no one else in their lives showing them Jesus. This is an important calling, and I'll stress again the importance of spending time in fellowship with Jesus Christ, pouring over His Word to understand how He is asking you to walk out your ministry and make disciples of Christ. Loving people, offering a helping hand, and human kindness are just a few ways you are called to actively walk out your ministry while executing your daily work responsibilities.

Everything you do in the workplace, from cleaning up after yourself in the break room to the quality of the work you produce, reflects the presence of the Lord Jesus Christ in you. Whether you are a manager or an associate, do everything you do as if doing it for the Lord. Some of us are called to be bold in marketplace ministry; others are called to quietly live out the character of Christ. I can't tell you which calling is yours, but the Holy Spirit within you can. You walk out your assignment as the Lord leads you. But remember, not everyone around you is waiting for you with open arms to preach the gospel and save them. There are many who will desire to trip you up and thwart your ministry.

> **The knowledge of the secrets of the Kingdom of heaven has been given to you, but not to them. Whoever has will be given more, and they will have an abundance. Whoever does not have, even what they have will be taken from them. This is why I speak to them in parables: "Though seeing, they do not see; though hearing, they do not hear or understand." (Matthew 13: 11–13)**

We are called into the marketplace for a Kingdom purpose, and now we're considering that we aren't always supposed to share our God with just everyone. This is an important concept that requires time with the Lord and discernment from the Holy Spirit to guide each step of the way. Some people who you are uniquely positioned to impact for the Kingdom will be doubters and will come against you—and the Lord will still lead you to minister to them by walking out your Christian calling. There are others, however, who will seek to destroy your mission. God always wins. We know that. But you have to be connected to, and be listening for, the direction of the Lord to know what God is calling you to do in each situation. Sometimes, he'll guide you to hide your light. Other times, he'll supernaturally protect you by causing confusion to those who would seek to trip you up and harm you.

As a leader in a large secular organization, I had the opportunity from time to time to speak to teammates gathered in large groups. On one such day, there were 300 gathered for a specific business purpose and we were enjoying lunch together. When it came time for me to give what I planned to be a state of the business update, I walked to the center of the room in order to get the best acoustics and be in the center of the gathered team. What had come to be recognized by me as the anointing of the Holy Spirit came upon me, and I thought, *Okay Lord, what are you going to say?* I became a vessel for the next few minutes while the Lord stressed the importance of the path ahead of us, that operating with integrity every step of the way would be key in moving forward. I offered assurance that our significant success was a result of God's protective hands of provision over us all. It was a speech that inspired many, and teammates talked about it for a long time. Two additional significant things happened as a result: First, believers recognized that the Lord was moving our secular workplace to do great and mighty things, and second, non-believers were completely unfazed with what was a pretty fiery "sermon". The Lord lifted those who needed reassurance, and protected His purpose and His plan by not making it obvious to non-believers. Discern when the Lord is using you and trust that if you faithfully follow His lead, He'll protect you—regardless of the outcome.

In chapter three I described my "Joshua rocks". I kept this "Joshua rock wall" on a whiteboard in my office. It was a written list of key phrases, and sometimes names, dates, or numbers; these were all reminders of business strategies or decisions that came to me without great difficulty, and that, when implemented, delivered incredibly successful results. The list hung for all to see. I recognized these as "Holy Spirit Business Ideas", but the list wasn't labeled as such. Everyone who came in my office asked about the list. The list was "encrypted", written in shorthand. It was written *by* me as a reminder *for* me. Without explanation, it meant nothing to anyone else. Each time I was asked, I would wait for proper discernment before going too deep into the story of Joshua and God parting the Jordan River and my "Joshua rock wall". Sometimes I would simply say, "It's a list that reminds me of some business decisions that worked out great." At other times, it would lead me to witness to the person about God's faithfulness, Joshua's journey, and the gospel of Jesus Christ. My rock wall was one of my best tools for witnessing of God's faithfulness. It also certainly could have caused chaos in the hands of someone who intended to do harm. Discernment was a key protector of this "pearl".

The greatest satisfaction I ever experienced in the workplace was to have someone come to my office door and sheepishly say, "Will you pray for me?" Sometimes I think they probably wanted to give me their request and leave so I could pray, and sometimes I would do just that. But more common was that after doing my Holy Spirit "gut check", I would invite them in, listen to their concern and, with permission, would put my arms around them, bow my head, and pray right there in the office for them.

One day, while my head was bowed, a young man came to the doorway and saw me praying over a teammate. Before I realized he was there, he walked away. Later that day, he returned to my office, and I invited him in. He told me he was originally coming to me for advice, but after he saw me praying he wondered if I would pray with him about an issue he had. I felt honored and, putting an arm around him, prayed as he wept. (As another sign of God's faithfulness, I came to recognize these godly assignments as moments in time that were gifts from God for me. In return for just a small token of obedience of lifting up a teammate in prayer, the Lord gave me confirmation that my ministry was making a difference in the lives of people who needed Jesus Christ.) There were other times, however, when someone might reference this prayer practice and the Holy Spirit led me to believe the inquiry was mocking rather than genuine. In those cases, I would simply move onto business discussions or otherwise keep the conversation secular. You'll need to practice your "gut check" of discernment to understand in your setting where boldness might be ordained by God and when it might be a trap of the enemy meant to harm you.

> **Instead, God chose things the world considers foolish in order to shame those who think they are wise. And he chose things that are powerless to shame those who are powerful. (1 Corinthians 1:27)**

Sometimes the Lord will give you concepts and ideas that just don't make any sense when applied to the world's business rules. These are the most difficult ideas to execute. The ideas will require your most creative approach when delivering them to people in authority who don't know the Lord. Pray without ceasing and walk in faith. Sometimes man opposes the Lord's ideas. This doesn't change God's plan, nor does it reflect your obedience in attempting to execute upon it. Always be open to His next great idea and trust that He's ultimately in control, regardless of the nature of your circumstances or resistance from man. Be obedient to the Lord by voicing what you believe is correct, and bring honor to your position by carrying through whatever plan is ultimately decided upon. In other words, if you believe the Lord is leading you in one direction, but you lack the authority to make that move, voice your ideas and respectfully follow the direction of your leader. Nothing surprises God. He knows who will be obedient, and he knows who won't listen. Trust that his bigger plan includes that failure to accept his plan. Perhaps there is a lesson for others in ultimate failure, or perhaps there is promotion for you for your obedience. Do your part, and trust that God is in control.

I do believe sometimes the Lord is testing his faithful by giving us these creative ideas that are difficult for other people to understand. Confidence in the Lord that comes from faith and a genuine desire to hear His voice and to obey it will give you the courage you need to attempt to execute the idea. If you believe the Lord is ordaining your success and creating opportunities where you will carry out your gifts and talents, then you must trust that His ways are not our ways. (Isaiah

55:8-9) My experience tells me this: When the crazy God idea was implemented, it worked every time and no one thought it was crazy when it was successful. When the crazy God idea was rejected, it was characterized as a crazy idea of mine. I rested in the knowledge that my obedience in trying was all God asked from me, and no matter what the result, my trust remained firmly in the Lord. The Lord isn't surprised when the world rejects His plan. God's concepts and ideas always line up with the Word of God, so "crazy" just means different than the world. God will never ask you to do anything counter to His Word.

> **For the word of God is living and active and sharper than any two-edged sword, and piercing as far as the division of soul and spirit, of both joints and marrow, and able to judge the thoughts and intentions of the heart. And there is no creature hidden from His sight, but all things are open and laid bare to the eyes of Him with whom we have to do. (Hebrews 4: 12-13)**

Ultimately, God will be the judge. Expect to be scrutinized practicing your faith in the marketplace. The lost will act lost, and you shouldn't expect anything else. I encountered many non-believers at my various assignments over the past thirty years in the marketplace, and one behavior is common to nearly all. When non-believers know prayer warriors are around, it is not unusual for them to seek out prayer support just to "hedge their bets." Let's face it—all of us can use some form of help. It was an honor to intercede for the lost who believed I might have a connection to God that they didn't have; it also was an opportunity for me to let them know that God is real, that He loves them, and that He listens to their voices, too. Our need as human beings to believe in something greater than ourselves, even if we haven't yet accepted the truth of Jesus Christ, is strong. The same people who criticize your faith as weakness will seek to tap into it if they think it might serve them well. That's your opportunity to witness in love and its confirmation of your purpose in the marketplace.

Don't cast your pearls among swine. But don't forget that without Jesus Christ, none of us are righteous. Love the lost; people are watching you as you do so. Lives will be saved. When your ministry is in the marketplace, you are called to be light in the darkness. Lead by example and show the attributes of Christ. Little things matter, so be an encourager, find more good things to praise than negatives to counsel on, and act with integrity. Pray without ceasing and give it up to God. In all you do, you're a warrior on a battlefield. After all, without Christ's love, and ultimate sacrifice for our sins, we're all pigs.

REFLECTION

> **We are made right with God by placing our faith in Jesus Christ. And this is true for everyone who believes, no matter who we are. (Romans 3:22)**

- How can you show Christ's love in your workplace in this politically correct world we live in?
- Think about times when you've had creative ideas that seemed to come out of nowhere. Did you hide them or try to implement them?
- How can you honor the pray needs of others in your workplace?

HOMEWORK

- Make a list all the "little things" you can do to make a difference in the lives of people you work with and to show the love of Christ.
- Journal ways that you might discern when the Holy Spirit is telling you to act and when He's telling you to guard your actions.
- Review the verses cited in this chapter, and write your thoughts in your journal regarding how you can listen to the prompting of the Holy Spirit in the marketplace.
- Continue to seek the Lord in reading the Bible everyday—the best way to know if our actions line up with God is to know His Word. Journal your plan and your successes.

CHAPTER SIX:
THE JESUS CARD

Finally, be strong in the Lord and in his mighty power. Put on the full armor of God, so that you can take your stand against the devil's schemes. For our struggle is not against flesh and blood, but against the rulers, against the authorities, against the powers of this dark world and against the spiritual forces of evil in the heavenly realms. Therefore put on the full armor of God, so that when the day of evil comes, you may be able to stand your ground, and after you have done everything, to stand. Stand firm then, with the belt of truth buckled around your waist, with the breastplate of righteousness in place, and with your feet fitted with the readiness that comes from the gospel of peace. In addition to all this, take up the shield of faith, with which you can extinguish all the flaming arrows of the evil one. Take the helmet of salvation and the sword of the Spirit, which is the word of God. And pray in the Spirit on all occasions with all kinds of prayers and requests. With this in mind, be alert and always keep on praying for all the Lord's people. (Ephesians 6:10–18)

Spiritual warfare or my own sinful nature—sometimes it's difficult to tell the difference, but the remedy and the preparation are the same. When I read the Bible everyday, listen to worship music in the car and at my desk, and have continuous conversations with the Lord, it doesn't get to me. On the other hand, when I skip these things, I find myself moody, easily offended, and likely to fall into sin. I like to think I can't start the day without coffee. After many years of struggling as a Christian in a secular workplace, I finally understand seeking the Lord is even more so a daily necessity.

- Sara L.

SATAN'S NUMBER ONE JOB IS TO GET PEOPLE disconnected from God and His purposes. From Genesis to current day, he has two tools that he uses to wage war effectively: distraction and deception. I can't stress enough how much you need your daily quiet time with the Lord to properly equip yourself for this battle. You'll need to arm yourself with battle gear, because at every corner, and when you least expect it, darts will come flying at you. Be on the lookout for evil, and recognize that the warfare is most often subtle. The constant conversation with God in your head will help you to recognize temptations and even ideas or concepts that aren't of God and that you should avoid. Spiritual warfare in the marketplace can take on many forms. Bickering and unrest among teammates, equipment failures, and miscommunication are just a few. Stay focused and take a step back. Phone a prayer friend. Rebuke the devil and he will flee. Just because you're a believer called to ministry in the marketplace doesn't mean life's going to be easy and without conflict. Expect difficulty.

I hope by now you understand why I'm a broken record, reminding you to find quiet time with the Lord each and every day. You must put on the battle gear before heading into each day's battle in the marketplace. Only then will you be able to withstand the attacks that will mount against you. I also recommend you identify another working woman of faith to be your prayer partner. I am fortunate to have such a woman who has committed her time and intercession to my business success for many years. This is a strong woman of faith whom I met in the marketplace many years ago when we were business peers. She later left the marketplace to become a full-time missionary. Nearly every Wednesday morning for years we prayed together over the phone, taking up a 7 a.m. "meeting" slot. When I found myself getting caught up in warfare, strife, or difficulties, she was a spiritual barometer and powerful intercessor who reminded me of my calling, my purpose, and that God was in control. I count it an honor that this woman believes her calling is to stand by marketplace ministers in prayer. Our weekly "meetings" kept me grounded, caused my faith to grow, and she was a powerful accountability partner in the workplace. Look around your network of working women and find a prayer partner.

You're going to encounter plenty of warfare when your ministry is in the marketplace. Remember, your calling is special, unique, and ordained. Because of that, expect warfare to go with the territory. If you understand this, you'll have a better sense of what motivates people or circumstances that are driving you crazy, and you'll be inspired to look at them in a more favorable light. Be aware of all the people and practices

Satan will use to get you off your godly game. Keep God in the center of your thoughts. You'll be able to spot the enemy before he defeats you. Satan does not want you to be successful in your ministry.

Expect that the closer you come to hearing the Lord and walking our your Kingdom purpose, the more you'll be tempted to sin. Consider Jesus' journey in the gospels. He enters the waters of the Jordan River to be baptized by John the Baptist. He is baptized, the heavens open, and the Lord proclaims, "This is my son, with whom I am well pleased." (Mark 9-13) I think we can all agree that is a tremendous spiritual moment in the life of Jesus. What happened next to Jesus should heed us warning. Jesus was *called into the desert and he was tempted by Satan.* From a spiritual high, Satan attacks. Spend some time in your quiet time thinking about this and about the weapon that Jesus used to counter every single one of Satan's attacks. He held scripture in his heart and recited it in response to every temptation. Makes seeking the Lord and daily bible study take on all new meaning, doesn't it? The Word is strength, truth, and protection and equips us to resist warfare attacks.

> **Blessed is the man who remains steadfast under trial, for when he has stood the test he will receive the crown of life, which God has promised to those**

> **who love him. Let no one say when he is tempted, "I am being tempted by God," for God cannot be tempted with evil, and he himself tempts no one. But each person is tempted when he is lured and enticed by his own desire. Then desire when it has conceived gives birth to sin, and sin when it is fully grown brings forth death. (James 1:12-15)**

We think of spiritual warfare as forces of evil that come against us. While that's true, I caution you: Beware of the obstacles you'll place in your own path as well. Sometimes spiritual warfare comes straight from within us in the form of greed, debt, or coveting earthly "stuff". If you allow yourself to get strapped with significant debt as you seek a bigger house, newer electronics, and bigger toys, then recognize that you may be tying your own hands and limiting your impact for the Kingdom. Debt will dictate your next move instead of allowing ministry to guide your path. You won't have the freedom to follow God's purpose if you're living well beyond your means. I am so thankful for my godly husband who has always had a keen understanding of this principle. Jim hates debt; God wired him this way. Even before we knew the Lord, Jim was a great money manager, and as a result, we've never lived beyond our means. Because of that, we've always had the earthly freedom to follow the godly purposes for our lives. Don't let the devil take you out of the game by racking up unnecessary debt.

Succumbing to the temptation of our sinful nature will also derail our progress in our Kingdom purpose. We must begin to resist temptation at the foundation by building our faith in Christ and by abiding in the Lord. Our energy, attention, and focus need to be spent practicing Jesus' command in John 15:4, "Abide in Me and I in you." Broken record, I know. Read the word, pray without ceasing, seek His voice and His direction, worship, then rinse and repeat.

> **Do not be afraid or discouraged because of this vast army. For the battle is not yours, but God's. (2 Chronicles 20:15)**

This verse is my go-to verse. Whenever I'm discouraged and feeling overwhelmed in the workplace, I remember my Kingdom purpose and who gave me the assignment, and I tell myself, "Oh, yeah, the battle isn't mine—it's the Lord's." Sometimes I need to remind myself of this several times a day. God will do the fighting. It is, after all, *his cause.* We will conquer, but not in our own strength. When you feel the fear welling up, remember this verse. The battle is not your own.

When you experience warfare, it's tempting to fight back in worldly ways. Learn to take the high road. This often means acting or reacting to a situation in a manner that seems inconsistent with how the world tells you to respond. As a believer, you constantly have to be aware of how your actions are perceived by everyone who is watching, friend and foe alike. Let others take the gutter. You will encounter this time after time as you are maneuvering your way through business and growing up the ladder. You will not find Kingdom advancement in the gutter. Quick satisfaction and perhaps even a momentary rush of "gotcha" will be outweighed by the disappointment of knowing you left an ungodly example for others in your wake. People are watching everything you do. Success will come the right way, and it's all the more satisfying knowing you didn't violate godly principles to get there.

Confront discouraging circumstances prayerfully and listen intently for the Holy Spirit's direction. Be careful of the sinful nature that lingers right under the surface. You will be attacked, and there are a hundred wrong ways that will come to mind quickly for you to react and retaliate, whatever the circumstances. This is another reason why seeking God's direction and reading the word every day is so important. You are stronger when the word of God is hidden in your heart and comes quickly to mind in times of trouble. Rebuke the devil, and he will flee from you. (James 4:7)

> **And no wonder, for Satan himself masquerades as an angel of light. It is not surprising, then, if his servants also masquerade as servants of righteousness. (2 Corinthians 11:14–15)**

The most prevalent spiritual warfare that I encountered in the secular workplace is what I like to call "people who play the Jesus card". Because I am bold in my faith, many people—associates, investors, business partners, executives—will, from time to time, talk about faith or calling or purpose or discernment in order to influence my business direction. As a marketplace minister called to be bold in my faith, this is my biggest challenge. The Lord highlighted this trap early in my leadership career. There was a new teammate who frequently came to me with lots of questions about God and faith. She was in a remote location and would bombard me with email inquiries, requests for phone meetings, etc. I answered her questions but had an underlying unrest about the vigor of her inquiries. After a short period of time, it came to my attention that this married teammate was entrenched in sin. I wondered if she was feeling conflicted and that was why she had so many inquiries about the Lord and faith. I was scheduled to travel to the location where she worked for a site visit, so I planned to meet with her to minister to her and perhaps guide her to the right path. The night before the meeting in my hotel room

I couldn't sleep. The Lord kept prompting me to get out of bed and open the Bible. I was obedient, but not finding scripture that was speaking to me, I'd put my Bible away and go back to bed, only to be prompted by the Holy Spirit to try again. Then the Lord led me to the scripture in Acts 16 where there was a demon-controlled young girl who kept interrupting Paul's ministry by screaming on the street corner the truth but whose presence was disruptive.

> **She followed Paul and the rest of us, shouting, "These men are servants of the Most High God, who are telling you the way to be saved." She kept this up for many days. Finally Paul became so annoyed that he turned around and said to the spirit, "In the name of Jesus Christ I command you to come out of her!" At that moment the spirit left her." (Acts 16:17–18)**

I read this scripture and had peace about what the Lord was trying to teach me. While this woman was asking spiritual questions, her purpose was to disrupt the marketplace ministry. The Lord revealed to me that I was about to walk into a trap of spiritual warfare. I suddenly had clarity that I was not to interact with her or attempt to mentor her at all. Instead, I was to release her from the company. With this understanding, I was able to quickly and restfully sleep. The very next day she left the organization on her own accord, before I even had the opportunity to run into her, and with no intervention from me.

Wrap yourself every day in the spiritual armor, and march head first into the battle, remembering it's the Lord's fight, not yours. He'll equip you, speak to you, confuse the enemy, prompt you to hear multiple times if you don't get it the first time, and ordain your journey and your ultimate victory. Warriors are in battles, after all.

REFLECTION:

We wouldn't be called warriors if we weren't in a battle!

> **You, dear children, are from God and have overcome them, because the one who is in you is greater than the one who is in the world. (1 John 4:4)**

- Are you living your life in a manner that leaves you available to follow God's plan?
- Are you arming yourself to resist temptations?
- How will you think differently of challenges in the workplace when you see them instead as spiritual warfare?
- How does it make you feel when you understand you're not alone in the battles you experience?
- Are there times when you feel like people are playing the "Jesus card" with you?

HOMEWORK

- Journal your plan for putting on the spiritual armor of God every day.
- Find a prayer partner to support you in the battle and commit to regular meetings. Schedule the meetings on your calendar.
- Continue to focus on your connection to God this week by seeking Him. Journal your plan in your notebook.

CHAPTER SEVEN:
FITTING IN

In fact, everyone who wants to live a godly life in Christ Jesus will be persecuted, while evildoers and impostors will go from bad to worse, deceiving and being deceived. But as for you, continue in what you have learned and have become convinced of, because you know those from whom you learned it. (2 Timothy 3:11–14)

I have been blessed to have a leader that didn't just "talk the talk" at work, but walked the walk. This dynamic was new and awesome to me and helped me embrace my faith fearlessly. There was no shame, and there were no feelings of being disobedient to the Lord by putting on one face at work and another when I wasn't. Being able to be faithful in all areas of my life has made me strong; no longer am I weak, hiding my beliefs in embarrassment. This leader's footsteps have imprinted themselves on my continued journey toward being one baby step closer to the Christian His sacrifice deserves.

—Lisa S.

Our world isn't getting friendlier to people of Christian faith. It is becoming more and more difficult to talk about faith in the marketplace, much less openly pray or talk to people about Jesus Christ. I understand the magnitude of the calling. So does the God who created you for an assignment such as this. The needs of the lost are great and we may well be the only face of Jesus that people around us ever see. You may be a lost sinner's only chance of accepting Christ and receiving eternal life. An important ministry for sure, carried out in an unlikely mission field of the secular workplace.

You need friends and colleagues who understand your calling—and that includes professional women and fellow Christian women. If you are fortunate enough to have a friend who is both, you are doubly blessed! Pray for godly female friends who are also working women. I've prayed this prayer many times, and God has brought me several. Once, in my quiet time, I was thinking about a woman I knew from work who was having some professional struggles as she grew in her role. The Holy Spirit revealed to me, "She's one of us." I took this to mean that God was revealing to me that she was a mature Christian. I was so encouraged, and the next time

I saw her I approached her and asked if she was a believer. She not only was a believer, but also a seasoned warrior with a powerful story of strength in the Lord. We immediately shared a godly connection of support and mentorship.

If you don't have an opportunity to fellowship with other female believers, you need to find or even create your opportunity to do so. We were created to be in relationship with other believers. Your faith will grow stronger when you fellowship with other believers and understand and support their walk while they understand and support yours. Ask the Lord to reveal opportunities for you to connect with other women who are believers in your workplace. I believe he'll send you a comrade or two and together your marketplace ministries will be even more powerful. Think also of how you carry yourself as a believer. Do others recognize you know the love of Jesus Christ? Don't overlook that there may be another woman of faith in the marketplace living out her Kingdom purpose, and she can't tell that you are her sister-in-Christ.

> **Though one may be overpowered, two can defend themselves. A cord of three strands is not quickly broken. (Ecclesiastes 4:12)**

It may be difficult as a working woman to find a fellowship of believers that works with your family and work schedule. It's not uncommon for churches to hold women ministry opportunities in the afternoon or right during dinnertime. Is there a scheduling void that you are supposed to fill? Perhaps there is no working women's ministry at your church because no working woman has started one? Are you supposed to start one? The thing that annoys you the most might just be part of your purpose. I have attended non-denominational churches for most of the last twenty years. My experience is that women with marketplace callings aren't really recognized in the doctrine that is lived out in the modern church. I am a firm believer that you shouldn't criticize what you aren't willing to work to change.

Think outside the box. Several years ago, when I was feeling especially lonely and feeling like the church we attended didn't understand the needs of working women, the Holy Spirit gave me a great idea to provide working Christian women a "place" to go for fellowship that would provide important support and friendship. This idea would provide structure, accountability, partnership, but wouldn't take these women away from their home and family, or interrupt their schedule. I started a working women's chatroom—a private "room" located on the internet where for several years we have held virtual meetings for an hour a week, after the kids are in bed, to do bible studies, book reviews, or chat about a daily devotional. This group has evolved into a tight-knit group of sisters. We've become each other's prayer warriors via email, and we're always accessible to each other electronically. From the very beginning, we called it a "guilt-free zone" because working women don't need more reasons to feel guilty. That means attendance each week is optional. I facilitate the group, and if I'm unable to attend, there are a few other mature Christian members who raise their hand to lead. Over the years, the Holy Spirit has led us to invite a few seekers, some baby Christians, and mature Christians to join. There are thirty-five members altogether, and on any given week you can find 5–10 of us online, encouraging and supporting one another in the struggles of life, based on the principles of Jesus Christ. At least one member came to know the Lord, and most have been inspired to seek Him in a deeper way.

All of us have benefited from the relationships we've formed with each other. We try to plan one "live" meal together each year in a restaurant, and from time to time, several of us get together to take a women's ministry retreat to recharge. We span several states, and some of our most loyal attendees have never met most of the rest of the group in person. We protect the privacy of the group by only allowing people to be personally invited by a known member after being approved by one of the facilitators. These are some of the most faithful women I know, and the assignment of shepherding this flock in some small way keeps me on track with my quiet time and prayer life. I am grateful for the revelation from the Lord that "fellowship" can mean something different than meeting in a church basement once a week.

Here's the bottom line: You're a strong woman, a leader; that's why you're in the pages of this book. Instead of saying there isn't a place of fellowship for you, create one. You never have to wonder if you're following your godly purpose when you do something that furthers the Kingdom of God in such a way. That's His perfect purpose for all of us. Find a group that fits your family's needs. If you can't find one, start one!

Because you're already feeling "different," you run the risk of feeling alone. Finding fellowship with other women who are believers will give you an anchor to your faith, give you prayer partners, and even offer an avenue of accountability. Don't skip this step fearing you don't have time to have friends. God intended us to be very relational human beings, and having friends is important to your sustainability in the marketplace and in your faith.

> **But in your hearts revere Christ as Lord. Always be prepared to give an answer to everyone who asks you to give the reason for the hope that you have. But do this with gentleness and respect. (1 Peter 3:15)**

You also need to connect with working women who don't know the Lord. The higher up the corporate ladder you go, the more likely you are to find yourself the only woman in the room. You have to find other similarly situated women to collaborate with in order to flourish professionally. These women may be inside your organization or in other companies. Finding the right network is important for growth and collaboration with business challenges, and it will provide an important environment where you can ask business questions and learn from each other's experiences. You should be able to find a working women's organization in your community or online. Identify a group that will provide an environment of support. Sign up for newsletters and attend events, as you are able.

If you have the ability and the opportunity, you may want to even consider starting a group like this in your own workplace. Starting a women's mentoring group that perhaps meets thirty minutes prior to work once a week or over lunch once every two weeks can make a big difference in the culture of your organization, and it will also expand your scope of influence. Anything you can do to support and participate in mentoring opportunities and to be intentional in creating women-to-women relationships in the workplace will benefit your entire organization. When you encourage women to share their experiences and collaborate on solutions, you'll lift the entire organization up.

Offering mentoring opportunities doesn't just serve those who are being mentored. This is also a great way for you to connect on a personal level with other working women. It's a great way to get to know people well, as the mentoring relationship creates an environment of mutual, honest sharing for the purpose of mutual growth. Whether you're the mentor or the mentee, you'll walk away from these relationships stronger. I mentor several women, and in every single instance, I can think of how I've benefited and grown from each of these relationships. One woman in particular, whom I had the honor of mentoring for several years, had an incredible backstory of overcoming significant adversity. Prior to our mentoring relationship, I considered her to be guarded and introverted, and I didn't accurately perceive her value in the workplace. I'm very glad she had the nerve to ask me to be her mentor! By interacting with her in one-on-one mentoring meetings, I came to see her as an extremely talented, creative professional with interesting, valuable, innovative ideas. Because of her personal history, she lacked the confidence to speak up and share her ideas, especially in crowded rooms. We were able to work together to create and execute strategies that helped her grow and that helped our workplace improve. As her confidence through the mentoring relationship grew, she dared to share her game-changing ideas with the team. Mentoring marries our natural capacity to be relational, to nurture, and to support with our professional capabilities. The payoffs are huge; sometimes there's a diamond in that rough!

In many professions, you may still be largely a woman in a man's world—and this is especially true if you're in a position of leadership. Sometimes you just aren't going to feel like you fit in. Earn respect by being excellent at your assignment. It's especially freeing to understand that you are where God wants you to be. With all the knowledge and comfort of your calling, don't hesitate to raise your hand, speak up, chime in, pitch new ideas, take on the extra project, and offer ideas that change the game. Support other women in the workplace vigorously. Encourage their success. If you are a leader, always look for opportunities to highlight women, especially those who are excelling at what has traditionally been viewed as male roles. People who are just really good at what they do are generally successful. Find a professional mentor and strive to be your best.

You can't do marketplace ministry alone. You need to find fellowship with other strong, professional, like-minded women. This is definitely one investment of time that will reap results of increasing your stamina and refreshing your soul. You'll find professional women of faith everywhere you go. Connect with one, or a few, and help keep each other strong.

> **In everything set an example by doing what is good. In your teaching show integrity and seriousness. (Titus 2:7)**

Another way to ensure you fit in is by being excellent in all you are called to do. Don't focus on the ways that you are different or disadvantaged. It's hard for people to criticize your performance when you're doing your best by using all the gifts and talents the Lord has given you. Whether people like you or not, think you're "different" or even "weird", it's difficult to reject someone who is just really good at what they are assigned to do. When you fulfill your work responsibilities with excellence, you make everyone else's job easier and that will give you favor.

Our community had a large church that was well known for its excellent orchestra. Each summer, the music director would throw a net out into the community and ask for interested musicians to come and practice and play in the orchestra for their holiday events. I had been an excellent musician in high school but hadn't really played the flute in more than thirty years. Regardless, I responded to the invitation thinking it sounded like fun. At the first practice, I immediately realized I had entered a group that took their gifting and their assignment very seriously. That first practice we plodded through the music, sight-reading, and occasionally being called on section by section to play. To say I was rusty was an understatement.

At the end of the rehearsal, the conductor left us with these parting words: "If you desire to be part of this orchestra, give it your best—not your leftovers, but your best. That means practice, practice, practice, and ask for help when you need it. Ensure your instrument is in tune, and work with all your might to get every note right."

After listening to that conductor, I realized that unless I was committed to being excellent, I simply wasn't going to fit in or belong there. I was pretty awful at sight-reading; the music was college level, and I had to work to be average, much less excellent. It inspired me to realize that if I could rise to this challenge, then it would be a great life lesson, teaching me that there was nothing I could not overcome if I committed to being excellent.

And so I chose excellence. I practiced and practiced and practiced, and something amazing happened: playing the flute came back to me after thirty-five years. My efforts encouraged those around me in the flute section to also be excellent. I offered a hand up to a high-school student in our section who needed rides to practice and another woman who really needed a new flute. By focusing on excellence, I inspired others to overcome challenges so they could be excellent, too. At first I didn't really fit in there, but by striving for excellence I earned myself a seat in the woodwind section. Striving to be excellent is great for so many reasons: It reflects all the best qualities of

Jesus, provides a powerful witness to others, and it allows us to fit in.

Do what God has called you to do to the best of your ability, following God's direction. Be excellent. Seek to be a great example of the love of Christ to others, and find a similarly situated woman to support who will in kind support you. This is a godly recipe for great success.

REFLECTION:

Sometimes you just won't feel like you fit in. You can wallow in that feeling, or you can find a network of business and Christian friends. If you find a few who are both, you win! Don't let your disadvantage be an excuse for failure or disobedience.

> **My prayer is not that you take them out of the world but that you protect them from the evil one. They are not of the world, even as I am not of it. Sanctify them by the truth; your word is truth. As you sent me into the world, I have sent them into the world. For them I sanctify myself, that they too may be truly sanctified. (John 17: 15-19)**

- Do an inventory of your personal and professional network. Do you have a support system for collaboration and support?
- How might you pray for a sister-in-Christ to be revealed? Journal your thoughts.
- Do you focus on being excellent in everything you do in the workplace?
- How could you mentor women in your workplace?

HOMEWORK

- If you don't have a professional mentor, dedicate this week to identifying one and exploring what that relationship might look like for both you and the proposed mentor. If you aren't mentoring anyone, is there a way you might create these opportunities in your workplace?
- Journal your prayers and petitions to the Lord regarding your network needs.
- Review women's ministry opportunities at your church, or consider ways you might meet this need for others if there is a need.
- In what areas are you convinced that a focus on excellence would make a difference?
- Continue to journal your plan and successes for seeking the Lord.

CHAPTER EIGHT:
JUGGLING ACT

Do nothing out of selfish ambition or vain conceit. Rather, in humility value others above yourselves, not looking to your own interests, but each of you to the interests of the others. (Philippians 2:3–4)

I worked for this marketplace minister in my first years in a secular corporate setting during some very transitional years in my life. It is clear that some of my growth and transition came because of the grace and discipleship I received in our workplace. There were times when my lack of experience and overall immaturity negatively affected my co-workers and my daily output. Rather than simply scold, groom, or discipline me for my attitude or actions, she showed me God's grace and forgiveness, while loving me and praying for me. I was blown away, because I expected (and probably even deserved) stern correction. She would not shy away from challenging her employees, but always in love and with the vision and intention of one who follows Christ. She would pray before making decisions. She would share life with you and welcome you into her own spiritual walk with vulnerability and honesty. Most importantly, she would openly proclaim the goodness of God to anyone her life touched. I am so thankful for our years together, and I know God's Kingdom has grown as a result of her faith and boldness. Now, as a wife and young mother with a strong marketplace calling of my own, I remember and apply many lessons from this mentorship.

—*Sarah N.*

GOD CREATES MARKETPLACE PURPOSES AND assigns them to certain women of faith in order to impact the Kingdom of God for the benefit of others. You fulfill this purpose while you are in the marketplace. This requires you to understand balancing the responsibilities you have. You are one person with one calling. God never asks us to do anything that is counter to biblical truths. If you are pouring all of your time and attention into your work and neglecting your husband or your children, you need to take a step back. That's not God. Balance your output appropriately; make your godly priority list. Time with God and your relationship with your family and your children are right there at the top. We always find time for things we care about—always. If you think you don't have time, then something less important to the Kingdom is taking up that time slot on your to-do list. Put your quiet time with the Lord *and* your marketplace calling in the proper place on your to-do list.

What happens if you leave work after an eight-hour day? If you don't know the answer to that question because you've never tried it, try it and see. Here's the closely held secret: nothing happens, except other people begin to wonder how they might also dare to leave after eight hours. If you're afraid that you won't get that promotion, or you won't get that assignment completed on time, or whatever pressure you're applying to yourself, then you've bought into the world's view of success.

You're reading these pages because you want to ponder God's purpose for your life. God's not asking you to sacrifice your God-given family responsibilities to fulfill your marketplace calling. Give the marketplace your very best *when you are in it*. And give your family your very best when you are home. If you can't get to a place where that seems possible, then seek the Lord's will for your purpose. I assure you that under no circumstances is He calling you to put your job priorities over your family. Remember, your life is one ministry, not two. Your family and your work do not come from two separate "selves". If you need to, now might be a good time to go back and review Chapter 3 and the Proverbs 31 woman.

On husbands:

> **Likewise, teach the older women to be reverent in the way they live, not to be slanderers or addicted to much wine, but to teach what is good. Then they can urge the younger women to love their husbands and children, to be self-controlled and pure, to be busy**

at home, to be kind, and to be subject to their husbands, so that no one will malign the word of God. (Titus 2:4)

If you're married, your professional purpose doesn't trump your devotion and dedication to your husband. Assignments are always better with a supportive friend; who better than your spouse? You must honor your husband as the head of your household, even if you are the person who calls all the shots at work. Trust, honor, and obey. The number one thing I've learned after thirty-five years in the marketplace and nearly thirty years of marriage is that my husband is my best friend, my best supporter, my best cheerleader, and my best partner in discerning the will of the Father in our lives. My husband deserves my best. That means my first fruits, not my last. If I had come to understand this early in our marriage, we would have certainly saved a lot of time that we spent instead on challenges. I didn't always understand this, but now I'm making up for lost time.

Enjoy your husband! Take time to reconnect if you're disconnected. Remember why you fell in love with him in the first place. Recreate some of your earliest exciting encounters. Shave your legs! If you wear t-shirts to bed, throw them out; lingerie is fun and pretty and comfortable if you buy the right brand. Make your bed, and make it a pretty, inviting bed! Devour your husband—he is the most important human being on this earth and the other half of your most important relationship. Your children will grow up and leave the nest, but this man will still be there by your side. Enjoy him!

Imagine the lesson to your sons and daughters that their parents not only love each other but also are *in love* with each other. The number one mentoring advice I give young mentees in the workplace is to honor, respect, nurture, and grow the relationship they have with their spouse. It's never too late to get back to basics. Have lots of sex with your husband. If you put half the energy into having a fulfilling sex life that you put into telling him how tired you are, you'd come to understand that there is nothing more rejuvenating than a healthy, sustained physical relationship with your husband. You'll both benefit from the extreme bond that exists in your marriage that frankly not enough marriages enjoy. Whatever you do to make your marriage stronger benefits you, your husband, your children, and your career.

There is a trend for successful women to become the primary breadwinner and, in a growing number of cases, for men to stay home and take on the traditional child-rearing role. This arrangement isn't counter to God's teaching. I couldn't find one verse in the Bible that indicated that men have to make more money than their wives, or that men couldn't stay home and be financially supported by their wife. If you find the Lord is calling your family to this arrangement, walk it out with mutual respect and understanding while you work through the kinks that will likely come in the form of external scrutiny and pressure. Your husband's important role as the leader of your household doesn't change. How the two of you work that out will be as unique as your calling to the marketplace.

Respect your husband. I hope your husband is a follower of Christ. But even if he isn't (and perhaps especially if he isn't), when you respect your husband you impact his self worth and self-confidence in important ways and show him the love of Christ. When you reverence him, notice him, regard him in high esteem, show him honor, and let him know you prefer his company over any other, its builds up your marriage and the Kingdom of God. When you value his opinion, admire his wisdom and character, appreciate his commitment to you, and consider his needs and values as important, you are building the strongest earthly bond and serving your God well. Reserve time and energy for your husband.

On children:

> **We train up a child in the way he should go, and when he is old he will not depart from it. (Proverbs 22: 6)**

I'm not certain that it is possible to live a mother's life without experiencing some amount of "mommy guilt" no matter what you are called to do. I used to think my guilt cup was full to the brim because of the hours I worked spending time away from my children, and that every failure or bump in the road they experienced was caused by me being a working mom.

Then God gave me a gift of grace. I had a memorable conversation with a woman who was talking about her own kids at a dinner party a few years back. Our youngest daughter was experiencing difficulties finding her own way at the time; I was especially guilt-ridden because I didn't know how to help her through what I knew intellectually was her own course of growing up. At the same time, I knew I was working a lot and thought that perhaps being away from me was the cause of her difficulties.

I didn't intimately know this woman with whom I was conversing, but I found her telling me a story that sounded oddly like my own. Her daughter was going through many of the same challenges our daughter was facing, so I listened intently. I know God creates "coincidences" purposely, so I expected He had a big message in this story for me. She talked for maybe fifteen minutes; it was clear that she needed an outlet to relate her story. She had no idea that I also needed to hear it.

When she finished, I asked one simple question: "Are you a working woman, or do you stay at home?"

She replied, "Well, that's the crazy thing. I've been home her entire life, and I don't know what I could have done differently to have altered this course for my child."

The Creator of the Universe let me know that we parent to our best ability, and then children make their own way. God has a purpose for each of our children, just as he does for us; their journey and their purpose are tied together and belong to them alone. We parent with love, devotion, guidance, biblical training, and support. Our children grow to make their own path, determined by a strong foundation coupled with their own choices.

Let go of your mommy guilt. Easier said than done, I know. But in case you need someone to give you permission to give it up, here it is. Your children will potentially have different qualities than those raised by moms who don't work outside the home; these qualities aren't better or worse—they're different. Our oldest daughter has uncanny abilities to adapt to any situation; she is strong-willed, confident, intelligent, and wise beyond her years. I'm confident she learned many of these traits in daycare, sometimes learning to fend for herself before she probably should have been asked to. She also has a great understanding of who she is as a marketplace minister herself. She doesn't want to work the hours I worked or make the sacrifices to family that I made in order to live her purpose. Rather, she has started her own business at a very young age in order to have the freedom to follow the Lord's direction. Following the biblical direction of no debt, she and her husband live wisely, well within their means, and use their God-given talents to execute a plan for family, faith, and success. She's smarter than I ever was, and I'm not convinced she'd have these qualities if she had spent all her formative years under my direct supervision.

When our first daughter was born, I stayed at home with her for three months before returning to work. During my pregnancy, I was convinced I would return quickly to my management position. I arranged daycare for her before she was born and had a good plan in place. But like most new mothers, I had no idea of the depth of love I would feel for a child and how convicted and conflicted I would feel about returning to the workplace. At the time, I felt I had no real choice but to go back to work. My husband and I were young, with dreams of buying a big home and traveling the world, and those aspirations required a two-income family. And so my mommy guilt began.

Our second child arrived five years later. By then I was accustomed to daycare and was well established at climbing the corporate ladder. The timing of the birth of our second gift from God and a key business milestone for my company didn't coincide very well. I went into labor the evening before an important board meeting and two days before the opening of an expansion location that I was in charge of. Praise God, our angel was healthy and, as she would prove to be throughout her life, easy going. When my daughter was two days old, she and I returned to work a few hours every day as I led the opening of that expansion project. In many ways, those busy and rewarding times together at work, with a newborn riding in a front pack (mostly sleeping on my chest all day) was great mommy/daughter time. I held her close and nurtured and nourished her, never missing a beat professionally.

Deciding whether or not to return to the workplace after having a child is the hardest decision any woman has to make. Because of technology, you can make a living from your home with the right business plan, making it difficult to decide whether to take a break from the workforce and jump off the corporate ladder. Only you and your husband, and God, know what's right for you and your family.

Don't wait until your maternity leave is ending to have serious discussions. I encourage you to sit down and talk it out before the baby is born. Use a flip chart or a white board to talk about your goals and your purpose, and identify where taking a break of a few months or even a few years might fit in the plan. Even if you are convinced you will return to work, chart out an unlikely plan "B" if you decide to take a break from the marketplace. I always encourage this discussion before the baby is born. Many first-time young moms in the workplace can't imagine this baby will make any difference in their career plan. Only when they hold him or her for the first time will they understand that leaving that baby to return to the office will be the hardest thing they've ever done. If you find yourself having this discussion four weeks into your maternity leave, I urge you to consider that your abilities, capabilities, resume, and calling won't disappear if you take a break and enjoy the only time you'll ever have to hold and mold this little one as a newborn. I will try to talk you into staying home nearly every time.

If you must return to work, make good plans early in your pregnancy. Don't sign any childcare contracts that can't be broken should you change your mind once your child is born. Find resources that share your family values, and talk to lots of existing customers. That means lots of phone calls to parents who use the daycare services that have made your short list, as well as pediatricians, etc. You'll have a better chance of feeling good about your decision to return to work if you feel like your child is in a great place receiving great care. Guilt doesn't serve you or your child, so give it up! You are doing the best you can to fulfill your purpose. Sometimes you'll get it wrong. Most times, you'll probably get it right.

Maybe you'll make one decision and then change your mind like I did. One of my favorite fellow believers in the marketplace is walking out this very difficult decision as I write this chapter. I have a great deal of respect for this young woman. She is bright, articulate, favored, and strong-willed. She has a bright career path and a heart for the Lord. She's pregnant with her second child, her career is on the fast track, and her faith is evident in all she does; she has it all figured out … or so it seems. I reached out to her to get her thoughts when writing this chapter. I figured she'd quickly rattle off some great insights! Instead, she indicated the more she attempts to juggle family, faith, and success in the marketplace, the less confident she is that she has important insights and advice. See, you're not alone. That believer knows she is called to the marketplace to make a Kingdom impact, but her struggle with obedience is real. One day at a time. Seek God's direction, review the busy list; lather, rinse, repeat.

This struggle of moms who work outside the home is real. The Creator of the Universe understands your challenges, and when you genuinely seek His direction, you'll find it—one day at a time. I cherish the time I had at home with my girls, and I cherish my calling to the marketplace as they were growing up as well. Your journey is part of the story that God is entrusting to you. Cherish the time you spend seeking His direction as much as you cherish hearing His voice, and He will make your path straight.

On others:

> **Then make my joy complete by being like-minded, having the same love, being one in spirit and of one mind. Do nothing out of selfish ambition or vain conceit. Rather, in humility value others above yourselves, not looking to your own interests, but each of you to the interests of the others. (Philippians 2: 1–4)**

Manage your time wisely, and likewise recognize your impact on others' time. As a top leader of a large organization, I was in the humbling position of influencing the lives of thousands of people by my example. I was completely comfortable walking out my godly purpose and that God was sustaining me. I was surprised and a little taken back at the impact of my every word. Not one word sat idle. Someone would pick it up and run with it. I would make comments off the cuff only to later find that someone implemented the comment as a directive. I once had small talk with someone in the elevator, and the person later told me it was a life-changing conversation for her. I quickly saw that my actions were mimicked, too, and this meant the hours that I kept at work. With our children now grown and my husband at the same company, we had the luxury of living out our godly purpose together as the primary focus of our lives.

We worked all the time, talking about work whenever we were together, strategizing, planning, and pouring ourselves into this exciting, growing, booming company. I loved the responsibility of running this large multi-state operation, and I loved the team. Every business decision I made would impact the thousands of lives that depended on the business to be successful—employees caring for their families and our tens of thousands of customers who relied on our service to deliver excellence to them. Because my brain was always "on", I found myself communicating at any time of the day or night with the leadership team. Believing transparent communication is key to success, I sent out weekly messages to all employees and updated the team on our opportunities and successes. I nearly always sent the messages on a weekend.

One day the Holy Spirit convicted me. I worked primarily with younger leaders who were at different stages of life than Jim and I. Most had young families and were juggling many responsibilities outside their significant career responsibilities. The team respected me. When I worked all the time, they felt the need to follow suit and work all the time too. In a quest to motivate and be transparent, I communicated a lot. If I wrote and sent an email on Sunday nights, people opened, read, and responded to the email on Sunday nights. My desire to be a strong, godly, dedicated, hardworking, transparent leader was actually stressing the team to emulate my work hours in order to show me their commitment. It was never my desire to have these folks take time away from their families on a quiet Sunday evening reading my messages; those messages should hold the same level of excitement come Monday morning! I was convicted, and I tried my best to make an intentional effort to stop communicating outside usual work hours. Once I came to this realization, I didn't stop working all the time—after all, Jim and I loved every minute of our assignments—but I did try to relegate my enthusiasm (as communicated to my team) to office hours.

As you work through understanding the balance of your marketplace purpose and your family time, be aware of others juggling similar callings and responsibilities. Respect the members of your family unit and theirs, and do your best—one day at a time. How you treat others is a powerful witness of who you are and of what the love of Christ means to you. Respecting their struggles and their boundaries is just the right thing to do. Being like Christ and respecting others is an important part of your ministry calling.

And finally, you:

> **Don't you know that you yourselves are God's temple and that God's**

Spirit dwells in your midst? (1 Corinthians 3:16)

Take care of yourself. In my fifties, I am physically fit and at my body's healthy weight for the first time in decades. I believe God has called me to focus on physical health so that I may run the rest of the journey He has in store for me. God has created you for a perfect purpose. He's given you all the resources you need to be successful, including time, talents, and opportunities. It's up to you to use all those resources wisely—and that includes the body you've been given to take you to the finish line. This isn't a diet and exercise book, but here are some truths: Sugar is poison. Processed foods aren't good for you. Exercise is good for you. There are examples of health in the Bible to emulate. Eat like Daniel. Walk like Jesus. That may be the only diet and exercise program you'll ever need.

You are God's temple. Remind yourself of this by putting sticky notes around your kitchen or in your pantry. Take five minutes to pack a healthy lunch to take to work so vending or fast food won't tempt you. Think about your body as your vehicle: Your ministry requires fuel and maintenance to keep it running smoothly. You'll be amazed (as I was) how much better you feel and how much additional energy you have just by cutting out processed foods, drinking sufficient water, and moving your body throughout the day.

There are many reasons to take care of God's temple that is our body. As with any kind of ministry, the people who we are ministering to will look for us to be examples of Christ and our Christian faith. God has given you an important assignment, and you'll need to have the appropriate level of health, wellness, and energy to carry it out. The Creator of the Universe made you, his masterpiece. He has convicted me that succumbing to an unhealthy lifestyle with fast foods and limited exercise and blaming it on a busy schedule was sin like any other. I have to resist the temptation and pray for His strength on a daily basis (sometimes hourly if there are brownies around). His mercy sustains me. By the grace of God, I will finish the rest of my race in good courage and good health.

You need to care for your spiritual self as well. Join a care group of some kind through your community or church to fellowship with other families. This opportunity for fellowship doesn't have to take away from precious family time. When our children were small, we were invited to a great care group with other families with kids of similar ages. New to our suburban Chicago home, we hadn't yet found a home church; we were attending a different church every Sunday. Then I answered the door one evening to quite a surprise: There, leaning on our doorstep, was a very tall woman dressed in rollerblades and full safety gear. She introduced herself as a neighbor from another block around the corner. She welcomed us to the neighborhood, handed me the fiction novel she had in her hand (it had clearly been her excuse for stopping), and then did the most amazing thing. She asked if we had found a church, and she invited us to her home to what she called a "small group" gathering. She told us this was a great way to meet neighbors and to fellowship. She asked if we had children and encouraged us all to attend.

I am so grateful for that woman today. She followed the prompting of the Holy Spirit and (what I would come to learn) stepped way outside her comfort zone to come to our door unsolicited and invite us to her home. We did attend that small group and from there found our church family where we would grow in our faith significantly. Not only did we get to fellowship, but also made lifelong friendships. These are friends we still remain in contact with many years later, and we've modeled the basis of our faith lives on what we learned from theirs.

When we later moved out of the Chicago area to Florida, we carried these experiences with us, along with a keen understanding of the importance of fellowship to the growth and sustainability of any believer. We always sought to belong to what we fondly call a "small group". As our careers progressed requiring us to move, connecting with a church body and finding a "small group" was always at the top of our list. If there was no family-friendly small group available at our church, we would start one, recognizing that other people desired fellowship and had a practical need to be able to bring their kids, too. We set the hours to meet the needs of families with homework and bedtime deadlines and either paid or assigned a babysitter to keep the large group of kids safe in another area of the house.

The bottom line is this: You must take care of yourself physically and spiritually in order to fight the good fight.

> **And I want women to be modest in their appearance. They should wear decent and appropriate clothing and not draw attention to themselves by the way they fix their hair or by wearing gold or pearls or expensive clothes. For women who claim to be devoted to God should make themselves attractive by the good things they do. (1 Timothy 2:9–10)**

How you present yourself matters to the way people accept your actions and your words. If you really want to dress for work the way you dressed to go out at night when you were in college, then you might want to skip this chapter. There are a lot of dress options that I've seen in the workplace that don't make sense to me: professional women in leopard-print dresses and three-inch heels; low-cut blouses, fishnet stockings, spaghetti straps and flip-flops. (Yes, I've seen all of these in the workplace.) I must admit it still annoys me to see a young woman in the marketplace using her physical attributes to advance her career.

I understand why some women do it—it works. It's effective. It gets you noticed. The marketplace is still largely a man's world, after all. But it's not the way for a godly woman to present herself, and if your God-given purpose is to be in the workplace, God isn't asking you to violate His principles of modesty and self-respect to be successful there. Sometimes we are our own worst enemies as working women. We desire to be recognized as smart thought leaders while dressing in a manner that highlights sexuality. Be careful of sending competing messages to male counterparts who still largely outnumber women in leadership positions in the corporate setting.

There is a growing trend that suggests women buy a number of the same suits or work clothes, such as a plain black or grey suit, and dress up the common garment with different accessories. After all, that's essentially what businessmen have been doing since the beginning of time. It's an interesting idea. It certainly would save us time getting ready in the morning! I've been in the workplace long enough to know that if the idea did catch on, there would still be some hold-outs who wouldn't participate, and their clothing would be the only thing anyone noticed that day. I'm not suggesting you adopt that strategy, although it's intriguing (and the older I get, the more I like it). I don't care what you wear to work, but I do want you to know that it matters to your reputation and how you are perceived, even if you don't think that's fair. If you wear low-cut blouses that expose your cleavage, men and women will draw conclusions about who you are; if you wear what I fondly refer to as "hooker heels", again, men and women will draw conclusions about who you are. Think of your clothing as an important part of your personal brand for your ministry!

One young woman who worked in my office years ago was bright, beautiful, and extremely smart and capable. She wore short skirts, four-inch heels, and blouses with very low necklines. Animal prints were the mainstay of her wardrobe. She confided in me one day that she didn't think she was ever seriously considered for promotions. I began to mentor her, and business attire became part of our discussions and our strategy for change. As a single mother, she was concerned that she couldn't afford a new wardrobe. We researched consignment shops in the wealthier areas of a nearby city; over time she was able to put together a classy, professional wardrobe fit for any female executive. I saw her confidence grow; she began to act more assertively as her style changed. You could see her self-confidence rising and her professional demeanor improve. In time she was promoted and even entered a graduate degree program as her confidence grew. For the first time in her life, she understood that her value was not in her beautiful physical appearance. She was a bright, talented, gifted child of the most high God.

Keep your private parts private, and seek to be judged on your capabilities, not your physical appearance. You can call Timothy 2: 9–10 outdated, but you'll find human resource experts follow it when giving advice to job applicants. And in case you were wondering, leggings aren't pants and have no place in the workplace unless you work in a fitness club.

REFLECTION

When you're reflecting, think about where God's priorities are calling you to be.

- Are you devoting the right amount of time to your marriage and your husband to ensure he knows he's at the top of your list?
- What areas cause you to feel "mommy guilt"?
- Are you taking care of the vessel God entrusted you with?
- Are there areas where you might be encroaching on other people's family time?

HOMEWORK

- Make a list in your notebook of all the things you need to "get done" this week. Which things take away time from your calling? Reflect on your Jesus/Others/You responsibilities list. Are your priorities straight?
- Revisit your "Busy List" from chapter two and compare it to the list you just made. Did you successfully clean it up or is it growing again?
- Think about ways you can keep your responsibilities in the right order and the list the right size. Journal your plan to continuously reflect and modify your "Busy List", then stick to it!
- Continue to seek Him! Journal your successes in your notebook, and tweak your plan as needed.

CHAPTER NINE:
FOR SUCH A WRETCH LIKE ME

I thank Christ Jesus our Lord, who has given me strength, that he considered me trustworthy, appointing me to his service. Even though I was once a blasphemer and a persecutor and a violent man, I was shown mercy because I acted in ignorance and unbelief. The grace of our Lord was poured out on me abundantly, along with the faith and love that are in Christ Jesus. Here is a trustworthy saying that deserves full acceptance: Christ Jesus came into the world to save sinners—of whom I am the worst. But for that very reason I was shown mercy so that in me, the worst of sinners, Christ Jesus might display his immense patience as an example for those who would believe in him and receive eternal life. (1 Timothy 1:12–17)

As I grew as a Christian and a working woman, I would remind myself that while physically I am working for man, spiritually I am working for the Lord. God placed me wherever I have been professionally for His purpose, and even though I may not understand completely, it is His will, and He is the One I serve. My work is for the glory of God."

—*Laura W.*

THE GREATEST THING ABOUT WALKING OUT YOUR godly purpose is that it isn't complete until you take your very last breath. Every day is a new day to focus on Him and do it better than you did the day before. Just when you think you've figured out exactly where God's taking you, your story will take an unexpected turn and get even better! I have been so incredibly blessed to have a number of women tell me that my story has had a significant influence on the story God's writing in *their* life. I thank God that He can use a wretch like me, and He'll use you in similar ways if you let Him!

Tarsha is one of my very favorite people. The Lord placed her under my marketplace ministry when she was a young woman just starting in the business world. What an honor to be able to mentor her professionally and to learn years later that spiritually she had benefitted as well, in ways I didn't even know:

I was not brought up in a religious home. My mom said she had it shoved down her throat so much that she didn't want to do that to us, so she never "assigned" us a religion. That always kind of made me feel lost, like I wanted to belong to something. I met you at work when I was trying to figure out who I was and who I wanted to be. I had moved far away from home and was going through a very difficult and confusing time. I felt alone and lost. Although you didn't know what was going on with me personally, you suggested I look to God for answers, or that maybe God could help me. You never pressured me about what to believe, you just simply put it out there that if I'd seek to know whether or not He was real, I'd find the answer.

I asked God every day to come into my life more and to just be patient with me if he was real. And I would thank Him everyday for doing exactly that. Now I pray every night. I go to church. I talk to God on my drives, and I thank Him constantly for the blessings He has bestowed upon me. My faith is like the Northern Star: No matter where I am, I always have something to guide me home. It means I'm not lost anymore. My faith means leading a better, more purposeful life and presenting that same life to my children. It goes to show that you just need a faithful spark to ignite a fire. I will forever thank you for being the spark I so desperately needed to light the fire of God inside me. To get that in my workplace was amazing.

Our God is so faithful. He uses our imperfect witness and best effort obedience to bring souls into the Kingdom. You have the opportunity to impact others for the Kingdom of Christ in a most personal and profound way even when you think you're making no difference at all. When your ministry is in the marketplace you will be the light of Christ for people who have no paradigm to seek Him. For some you may be their first personal interaction with a believer. Your every action plants a seed that God will water as He draws the lost toward Him.

> **If we confess our sins, he is faithful and just and will forgive us our sins and purify us from all unrighteousness.**
> **(1 John 1:9)**

I pray my story in the marketplace, when it's told at the end of the day, will be one of obedience and Kingdom purpose. I also hope I haven't made marketplace ministry sound easy. That was not my intent. I'm fully aware of the weight and magnitude of the calling. God has certainly blessed my journey and walked before me in spectacular ways. That doesn't mean I hear His voice clearly every second of every day; it doesn't even mean I remember to *listen* for Him every day! I'm painfully aware of the times I've been out there on my own without His direction. I know I've gotten it wrong plenty of times. I've had to repent often. I've also had to pray (more times than I care to admit) for the Lord to place someone else in a person's path to be Jesus to him or her because my interaction with that person wasn't very Christ-like. Thank you, Jesus, for washing away my sins through the sacrifice of your blood, and for repentance!

Dying to your own sinful self must be a daily—even a second-by-second—exercise. When I forget to seek Him first, or forget to put on the spiritual armor, or forget to just be patient and wait for direction from the Holy Spirit, I easily wreak havoc on those very people I've been called to shepherd. We must never be satisfied with failure. We must seek God at all times. Each and every interaction may be the last chance a lost person has to accept Christ as their Lord and Savior before they meet their maker. When you get it wrong, repent, recommit, and pray for the Lord to transform you and to give you the heart of Christ. If you strive to seek Him every day, pray without ceasing, put on the spiritual armor, and walk with a heart that desires obedience, you'll probably get it right more times than you get it wrong.

> **...But those who wait upon the Lord will renew their strength. They will soar on wings like eagles; they will run and not grow weary, they will walk and not be faint. (Isaiah 40:31)**

I don't always wait for the Lord to speak before moving. I sometimes find myself talking to the Lord, saying, "I'm going this way. You coming?" After all, I reason (I can always reason away sin) marketplace ministry is a fast-paced calling and decisions need to be made on the spot. Warriors are by definition brave and experienced soldiers. There's nothing easy about being brave, and experience comes by doing. Then I'm convicted, and I repent of my prideful spirit, and I (hopefully) get behind the Lord instead of in front of him and carry on. I've had a lot of practice rattling off the excuses for getting ahead of God. Don't fall into that trap. There's a very fine line between sinful pride that God would call *you* to such a place of influence and godly humility to know that He is the one in charge. You are not alone in your struggle to get it right. If you seek His guidance in all things, God will use you in mighty ways, especially when you least expect it. My dear friend Carol is another marketplace minister—a solid woman of faith who I rely upon for support and intercession; we walk similar professional paths and use each other as (sometimes frequent) accountability partners. Here's one of her favorite got-it-wrong-then-got-it-right God stories:

Business travel is not for the faint of heart; it is filled with detours and delays, which are impossible to control. For the "Type A" personality, loss of control between wherever you are and your destination (or goal) can quickly test your character. Recently I was stranded by my favorite airline in an airport for over thirteen hours. Sadly, I growled at the ticket agent who eventually "blessed" me with a 10:50 p.m. flight to my destination. I walked away totally in the flesh, muttering, sputtering, complaining, and feeling sorry for myself.

As I trudged through the airport, I decided dinner might improve my situation. I quickly found myself sitting at a large high-top table with twenty other weary travelers who were mostly likewise stranded. I hadn't been seated five minutes before I realized the woman next to me was texting and crying, texting and crying. Yikes, I really wanted to move! I looked over at her out of the corner of my eye and saw she was wearing a cross bracelet on her wrist. I realized I had to a choice to make: wallow in my own self-pity (which I really wanted to do) or try to minister to this sister in Christ in the middle of the airport.

I have a very close friend who is an evangelist like no other I have ever known. She never hesitates to expect God to use her, anywhere, anytime, with any stranger, and especially when she travels. Her example immediately came to my mind, convicting me. Even though I didn't feel like it, I made eye contact with this crying stranger.

Through her tears, the woman apologized and said, "I am so sorry. I just found out my mom's cancer has come back, and I don't know how I'm going to get through this." I immediately reached over and laid my hand on the cross she was wearing on her wrist.

"I do," I said. We spent the next hour talking about her real sorrow: knowing her mom didn't have a relationship with Jesus and was now facing a terminal diagnosis.

I encouraged her to continue to share Jesus with her mom at every opportunity, trusting God for the outcome, just like my evangelist friend would do.

As we parted with tears and hugs in the middle of the packed airport restaurant, she told me, "I feel like God sent you here just for me today. You let me know God sees me."

That night, as I asked God to forgive me for my terrible attitude with the ticket agent, I also praised Him for using what little I had to encourage another. In reflection, I realized several people around us at the large table had listened to our conversation and watched our interactions. What an amazing God! In spite of my terrible attitude on that "wasted" day, He let my favorite airline "arrange" His appointment for me—an appointment that had an eternal goal.

Carol could have thrown in the towel and wallowed in her annoying circumstances, her disadvantage, and even her disobedience that day. Instead she views every single second of the day as a chance to turn and get it right. She is a faithful servant of Christ and a powerful marketplace minister. She is actually an able witness of what it looks like to wait upon the Lord, but when she finds herself ahead of God, she doesn't get discouraged—she refocuses on the throne and makes an impact for the Kingdom, even in her imperfection.

> **Do you not know that in a race all the runners run, but only one gets the prize? Run in such a way as to get the prize. Everyone who competes in the games goes into strict training. They do it to get a crown that will not last, but we do it to get a crown that will last forever. Therefore I do not run like someone running aimlessly; I do not fight like a boxer beating the air. No, I strike a blow to my body and make it my slave so that after I have preached to others, I myself will not be disqualified for the prize. (1 Corinthians 9: 24-27)**

Just like Carol's powerful example, think of your life in the context of obedience, second-by-second, minute-by-minute, and day-by-day. Whether you are in a support position or leading a company of thousands, whether you're praying with a believer or delayed in an airport on a busy travel day, you are called to make a unique and important impact on the Kingdom in each position and every circumstance you find yourself in. God uses all kinds of circumstances to begin a powerful assignment, like meeting your next employer while standing in your bathing suit in your front yard or meeting a sister in need at a restaurant table in circumstances made possible only by an extended airport delay.

Be certain to keep an open mind! Make your plans, but make certain you recognize they are just a reflection of your best guess of what is to come based on what you know right now. You never want to be so focused on your plan that you miss God's opportunities that spring up in ways only God can fashion. Remember, we're seeing just one thread in the tapestry; God sees the completed masterpiece.

Your godly calling is just that: *your* godly calling. This is not an aimless venture without a roadmap or plan. The Creator of the Universe has assigned YOU to the marketplace where you will fight the good fight for a Kingdom purpose in intentional and powerful ways. Each calling is unique, and yours will be different from mine. Keep your focus on the things of God, and do your best to discern His leading. Walk in obedience and plant seeds. God will water them and make them grow. You know how to prepare for the good fight. Seek God in all things. Read His word. Pray without ceasing. Listen to the prompting of the Holy Spirit. Get in the fight, warrior. There is no more honorable battle than this battle for souls.

Every circumstance, every interaction, and every situation has potential, purpose, and meaning. We're not expected to be perfect in the execution of our calling. We are expected to be willing. May you hear the Shepherd's voice clearly, and may you have the confidence and courage to walk out His commands. **Let the redeemed of the LORD tell their story! (Psalm 107:2)** God is trusting you with a story. Make yours a great one of obedience, servanthood, and faith that God will use to accomplish His purpose. God sees your faithfulness. He knows your heart. Fall into His arms and offer up your dreams to Him. He will guide you, direct you, provide increase and favor to you, and bring you peace. For such a time as this.

REFLECTION:

God is trusting you with a story. Are you writing that story *by faith?*

- How does seeing your calling as a marketplace calling change how you'll view your work?
- Do you see yourself as a warrior on the battlefield?
- Can you think of times of frustration where you may have missed a ministry opportunity, like Carol's example? How can you be ready for these kinds of opportunities?

HOMEWORK

- Go to Hebrews Chapter 11 in your bible. Circle each time in that chapter that you see the words "By faith". Anyone who comes to God must believe *by faith* that He exists and that He rewards those who seek Him.
- Look back in your journal entries you've made since reading this book. Can you see your "Joshua Rocks" that the Lord has revealed? Can you see evidence that you hear His voice?
- Continue to plan and schedule time with the Lord every day. Your marketplace calling depends on it!
- Let the redeemed of the Lord tell their story. (Psalm 107:2) Journal *your* marketplace ministry story and review it often, letting it refresh you along the way!

ABOUT THE AUTHOR

As a healthcare executive and evangelical Christian, Dotty J Bollinger has boldly served the Lord in the secular marketplace for nearly three decades, and attributes her professional achievements to the spiritual foundation on which she has built her career. Driven by conviction, she is passionate about mentoring professional women, and enjoys coaching them toward their kingdom success in the marketplace and at home. As a nurse and an attorney, Dotty served as SVP of Risk Management and General Counsel for Horizon Bay Senior Communities and most recently as President and Chief Operating Officer for Laser Spine Institute. Today, along with husband Jim, the Bollingers serve healthcare practices all over the United States with their consulting firm. She and Jim are parents to Ashley, Sara and son-in-law Kevin, and live joyfully in Gatlinburg, Tennessee. In their free time they find rejuvenation and inspiration by hiking, camping, cross-country skiing, working the land, and enjoying the breathtaking views from their cabin in the majestic Smoky Mountains.

Printed in Canada